APOLOGETICS FOR TWEENS

*How to save your children from doubts and
unanswered questions about Christianity*

5ᵀᴴ GRADE LESSON CURRICULUM

ISBN: 978-1-947844-02-5

THOMAS J. GRIFFIN

June 2017

Please read the Leader's Guide first before the curriculum to understand what is included, how to use the curriculum, and importantly the background and purpose for the curriculum as well as real world stories that emphasize the need for apologetics with our youth. To summarize here for you, the curriculum includes a weekly scripture lesson and apologetics lesson for a school year. It also has some recommendations for activities, contests and games as well as top questions and answers about the Bible and Christianity that came up over a twelve year period.

Resurgens

www.resurgensconsulting.com

ATHANATOS
PUBLISHING GROUP

www.athanatos.org

CONTENTS

5TH GRADE LESSON INDEX

5TH GRADE LESSONS

Scripture blurb	Apologetics blurb
School Year Month	
AUGUST (partial – beginning)	
Conviction	Do you know why you believe?
Conviction2	What is truth?
Abraham & Isaac	Law of opposites
Joseph sold	God exists part 1
SEPTEMBER	
Joseph in prison	God exists part 2
Pharaoh's dream	God exists part 3
Moses	God exists part 4
Adam & Eve	Why God gave us free will
OCTOBER	
Moses is called	Bible reliability part 1
Joshua & Caleb	Bible reliability part 2
Battle of Jericho	Bible reliability part 3
Read the Word	Is the Bible true?
NOVEMBER	
Samuel selects David	Who was Jesus?
Stepping in	Do Islam and Christians worship the same God
Other religions	God plays no favorites
Adjust your attitude	Evidence review
DECEMBER	
The Christmas story	Prophecies
David & Jonathan	Evidence for the Resurrection
Hope	Mormons, JW's
The gift is born	Was Jesus born of a virgin?

JANUARY	
	Apologetics review
Self-control	Islam overview
God loves you	Why does God not destroy evil?
Do your part	Grace vs good works
FEBRUARY	
Creation	Young earth or old earth?
Jesus amazed His critics	Top criticisms of Christianity
	The Shroud of Turin
Be kind to family and friends	Meet the skeptic
MARCH	
Patience	Who wrote the NT?
Don't have a cow	NT authors part 2
Passion of Christ	Did Jesus really die?
Faith	Was Jesus really resurrected?
APRIL	
	Evidence for the Resurrection
The visit	Resurrected body or spirit?
Persevere	Trinity
The Ascension	Second coming
MAY	
Be content	What is needed for salvation?
Do not covet	Prayer
Don't look back	Justice vs mercy
Is more better	Why all the Bible versions?
JUNE	
God is love	What does it mean to be good?
Parables	Why evil?
Friends love each other	What is heaven like?
Intercede	How does God hear 2 billion prayers?
JULY	
Stephen preached	How to share the gospel
Saul's conversion	How does salvation work?
	New Jerusalem
Be thankful	What do atheists believe?

AUGUST (partial – year end)	
Revelation	21 tribulation judgments
The assignment	How to use apologetics
EXTRA LESSONS	
Jesus gives hope	Did Jesus die and rise?
Alive forever	Comparison of worldviews
Loving my family	Is the NT reliable?
Jesus called disciples	What is required for salvation?
Don't worry	Worldviews - alternative
Honesty	Matching apologetics
	What about those who never heard?
	Are miracles possible?
	Did OT characters really live 900 yrs?

AUGUST LESSONS
(beginning year)

August in our church is a mixed bag with overlapping classes. Typically the first couple weeks are the completion of the prior year. Then it immediately transitions for the remainder of the month with the new class. So what follows below is the start of the new class. For the first couple months we typically introduce the basics of why apologetics and what it is, then the key major evidences that point to the truth of Christianity. From there we advance to related issues and then back to review key topics again, and so forth.

CONVICTION	
Scripture verses	Daniel 5
High level key topic	You can stand for what's right even when it's not popular

SCRIPTURAL LESSON NARRATIVE

Remember, you are fifth graders now and we expect you to act more mature as you prepare for middle school. Also, you have learned many lessons about the Bible and Jesus in the last few years. This year we will continue that but also help you understand why you should believe what you learn is actually true. That will help you overcome doubts about Christ and enable you to share with others who may not understand or may not believe.

FORMAT

1. Candy for Bible and word search – 1 each bowl – finish by 9:15

2. One rule – Respect, for teachers, for each other, for God's house

3. Lesson

4. Defending Christianity - apologetics

5. Activities

6. Closing prayer

7. Take home class notes

The topic is conviction. What is it? Conviction is when you stand up for something that is right and doing it in the right way. Of course you need to understand how to determine something is right first. The way to do that is to rely on God and His word. Jesus is an example for us and today's story is as well. Be aware that often when you stand up for what is right, it may not be popular, and you may be criticized, ridiculed, challenged and even attacked verbally or physically. When those times come, you can pray for help and trust God to help you through.

Today's scripture lesson is from Daniel 5. Why did God give us His word? It is to know Him and to know how to live our lives. In today's lesson we learn how Daniel stood up for what is right, even at great risk to his personal safety. This story is during a time when the Israelites were in captivity to the Babylonians. Daniel was one of the Jewish leaders assigned to keep the peace among the Israelites.

The new King, Belshazzar, held a great feast to celebrate their victory over Jerusalem. He used the stolen gold and silver cups they took from the temple to drink wine at his feast, praising the gold and silver as gods/idols. Suddenly the fingers of a man's hand appeared out of thin air and began writing on the wall next to the king. The king was petrified and asked his advisors to tell him what it said. They could not and he became even more terrified. The king's wife suggested he call Daniel, who was used by the previous king to interpret dreams.

The king offered Daniel riches and a position of power to explain the writing. Daniel refused the gifts but did tell him what the writing meant. Daniel explained that the previous king ruled with evil and terror over the people and did what he wanted. But God brought him to justice and took away his power, drove him away, made his mind like an animal and he lived in the fields with the animals until he accepted the one true God as ruler over all. He told Belshazzar that even though the king was aware of it he was acting the same. And so the hand and fingers were sent as a warning: Mene, Mene, Tekel, Parsin. It means that God has numbered the days of your rule and brought it to an end. You have been judged and found deficient. Your kingdom has been divided and given to the Medes and Persians. The king gave Daniel a robe and chain and made him third in charge for his interpretation. But that night the king was killed and Darius the Mede became king.

Do you see the risk that Daniel took? To give such bad news to a king might be certain death. But Daniel never swayed and trusted God. Could you do the same one day if your faith is challenged? Pray and stay connected to God so that you will have strength to do what is right if you have the opportunity one day.

DO YOU KNOW WHY YOU BELIEVE?

How many of you are saved Christians? Do you know why you are a Christian? Is it because your parents told you to go to church and believe what is taught? Or do you have good reason to really believe what you have been taught?

This is a critical question because as you grow older, tough questions and even criticisms about God, the Bible, Jesus and Christianity will be thrown at you. It may cause doubt and make you wonder if it is all true. Will you know how to respond? Will your faith stand up to challenges? Or will you move away from Christ? How do you know Christianity is true?

Fortunately, there is an area of Christianity that helps us to answer tough questions and criticisms so that we will know Christianity is true. We call this apologetics, which means defense. It comes from a Greek word and has nothing to do with being sorry for something. Throughout this year, we will present many pieces of evidence about key questions and issues to show you that Christianity is true.

Can any of you answer the following questions? We will help you understand during the year. Each week we will address something important about Christianity, other religions, science and the Bible, and many other areas.

What are life's most important questions and what is true?

How do we know God exists?

How do we know the Bible is true?

How do we know Jesus was resurrected?

How do we know other religions aren't true?

How do we know Christianity is true?

And many others.

CONVICTION 2	
Scripture verses	Daniel 1
High level key topic	Jesus showed us how to stand up for what is right

SCRIPTURAL LESSON NARRATIVE

This month we are talking about conviction. What is it? Conviction is standing up for something that is right and doing it in the right way. Of course you need to understand how to determine something is right first. The way to do that is to rely on God and His word. Jesus is an example for us. He found strength to do the right thing by knowing God's will. We can do the same but studying God's word. Be aware that often when you stand up for what is right it may not be popular and you may be criticized, ridiculed, challenged and even attacked verbally or physically. When those times come you can pray for help and trust God to get you through. And if you know what God's mission is, you can stand up for it. By studying the Bible you will know God's mission and through prayer He will guide you.

As examples, read Proverbs 14:2a; Hebrews 13:17; Matthew 22:37-39; Proverbs 17:17; Luke 6:31; John 3:16; Psalm 56:3; Ephesians 2:8; 1 Peter 2:17; Proverbs 21:3.

But it isn't enough to just know what the Bible says. You have to apply it to your life and live it. That is what it truly means to follow Jesus. Accepting Jesus is not enough. We need to try to be like Him.

Today's scripture lesson is from Daniel 1. Because the Israelites worshiped other gods and did evil but did not repent, God allowed the Babylonians under King Nebuchadnezzar to overthrow them. Many captives were taken back to Babylon. Some of the Israelites were chosen to help learn the language and train for 3 years to be the teachers to the Israelites. Daniel was one of those chosen. But the King required Daniel and his friends to eat and drink the Babylonian food and wine. But this went against the Israelites dietary rules. Daniel refused and asked to be tested for 10 days eating vegetables and water instead of meat and wine. At the end of the test, Daniel and his friends looked healthier than the others so they were allowed to continue. They were introduced to the King and found to be very valuable and served for several years. Will you obey God's word in times of trouble in your life even if it creates risk and danger for you?

WHAT IS TRUTH?

Before we can share evidence that points to the truth of Christianity, we must first understand what truth is and how we can know that truth is real. Many people in the world believe truth is more a matter of opinion. This creates a problem for our lives if that is the case. If truth is only opinion, we can know nothing for sure.

Truth is what corresponds to the facts and reality. And it is important to understand that if something teaches the opposite of what we know to be true, then that must be false. This is the first principle of logic, called the Law of Non-contradiction. Logic is the discipline of how to reason and think through problems. It is a critical principle because without it something could be true and false at the same time and this would create chaos.

But many people will tell you there is no truth, or that something may be true for you but not for them. These are false statements and must be understood and shattered.

We can know that the statement "there is no truth" is false because it defeats itself. Any statement that cannot meet its own claim is false. This statement claims to be true that there is no truth. Do you see the problem? It contradicts itself so it is false.

Here are some others:

- You can't know anything for sure.

  » Are you sure of that?

- You can't know anything.

  » Do you know that?

- No one can know anything about God.

  » Do you know that about God? To assert that God is unknowable is to say a lot about God.

- We can only discover truth by testing and experimentation.

  » Are you able to test that assertion?

- Apart from mathematics, we can know nothing for sure.

  » Is that statement a mathematical equation? No.

- All knowledge comes from observation.

  » Have you observed all knowledge? The assertion does not make possible its own ground of proof.

- All English sentences consist of four words.

  » Does that sentence contain only four words?

- We can know nothing about reality.

  » Do you know that about reality?

So, if we examine the facts, or evidence, it leads us to the truth. Although perhaps nothing can be 100% certain, this is part of how we live our lives and make decisions. But even if we find out later something is not true, that doesn't mean that the truth changed. For example, we used to think the earth was flat. Now we know it is spherical. But the truth did not change. Our understanding of the truth changed. Truth is something that is discovered.

Now that we know we can know truth about reality we can proceed to look at the evidence for Christianity.

ABRAHAM AND ISAAC	
Scripture verses	Gen 18, 21, 22
High level key topic	I should trust and obey because God has a bigger plan

SCRIPTURAL LESSON NARRATIVE

Today's lesson is about trusting and obeying God. God has a much greater plan for the world than just our little part. But we cannot see that grand plan so when things happen in our little piece of the world that we do not understand we must still trust that what we are doing somehow fits into God's overall plan. Perhaps when we get older we will see how it all fits (reference my call to ministry), or maybe once we are in heaven and all is revealed we will understand it. But if you continue to pray to God to guide your steps and your actions and ask forgiveness when you sin you will complete the part of God's plan that involves you. Nothing you do will thwart God's plan.

Our scripture today is about such an event. It continues the story of Abraham. Remember many decades earlier God predicted to Abraham he would have a son. Now at the age of 99 the Lord and some angels visit him and once again predict a year later he will have a son. His wife Sarah overhears and laughs about it because she is too old to have children. But a year later at the age of 100 Abraham has a son named Isaac (which means laughter). This is the first of many descendants who will all build great nations and be blessed through Abraham. This proclamation is called the Abrahamic covenant. A covenant is an agreement.

Abraham dearly loves his son due to all the circumstances. But over time he focuses too much on him and makes him like an idol. So God sent a test of his faith (read Gen chap 22). He asked Abraham to sacrifice Isaac on the altar. Abraham made the preparations and took Isaac and tied him on the altar and put wood over him to prepare to burn. But at the last minute the Lord brought forth a ram from the bushes for the sacrifice. Many do not understand why God would do all this or why Abraham would go along with it. But remember that God sacrificed His own son for our benefit, and Heb. 11:17, 19 indicate that Abraham might have believed God would raise Isaac from the dead even if he sacrificed him. In any case, Abraham did what God asked.

At 100 years old it must have been hard for Abraham to believe he would still have a son and that all his descendants would create the nations of the world. But all he had to do was believe the one thing that God told him: he would have a son. That was his part in the grand plan at that time. Remember he doubted God's plan at one point and had a child Ishmael with his wife's servant girl because he worried about having an heir. He should have trusted that God would deliver as He always keeps His promises.

THE LAW OF OPPOSITES
(NONCONTRADICTION – CAN'T GO AGAINST)

Remember that last week we discussed how we know there is actually truth in the world. Truth is what corresponds to the facts; to reality. We discover truth by examination of the evidence. To deny truth is to confirm it. When you say there is no truth you make a self-defeating statement and confirm there is such a thing as truth.

The reason we need to understand truth is because we could go through an all-day discussion of the evidence that shows Christianity is true but someone else might say, "Well it may be true for you, but Islam is true for me."

The next part of truth is to understand that anything that teaches the opposite must be false. This is a universal law of logic that applies to everyone at all times. It is not just some Christian idea. It goes back to the 4th century BC and was developed by Aristotle. This is a critical part of thinking because without it we cannot function in our lives. But many people ignore it for their own purposes.

The law of opposites (noncontradiction) says that two things that teach opposites cannot both be true at the same time and in the same sense or way. Let me explain this further and why it is important for Christians.

Many people have this idea that all religions could be true and that Christians are narrow-minded and insensitive and intolerant to think that we have the only truth about religion. They try to shame us to get us to agree that other religions might be true. Would it be important to know if other religions could be true? Of course, otherwise how do you know you believe in the right one?

Remember the simple example I used to show the law of opposites? Let's review:

- I.e. Ben in/out of room
    - >> I was looking at him at the time and he was all in the room
    - >> I didn't say part of Ben was in the room and part out
    - >> By definition, Ben means all of Ben

- But points out a piece of today's lesson – law of opposites/noncontradiction
    - >> Contradict means go against
    - >> Noncontradiction means cannot go against

- Law stated – two things that teach opposites cannot both be true at the same time and in the same sense

>> I.e. hot today but cold tomorrow, not hot and cold at same time

>> She looks hot today – hot temperature, hot in her looks – different sense

- Can something be up and down at the same time and in the same way? –no

- Can you get an A on the test but not get an A on the test? no

>> Let's say you cheated and got caught – that's not in the same sense

- Can something be dead and alive at the same time? – no

- Can you be on the airplane and not on the airplane? – no

>> Let's say you are standing on a model plane but not in an airplane

o Again that is in a different sense

- Can God be good and evil? – no

- If Christianity is true, can other religions be true? - no

Here's why it is important to us as Christians:

- What about religions – can they all be true? No

>> Could all be false – logically possible because they can be either true or false but not both

>> Cannot all be true because they contradict each other

o I.e. key belief of Christianity – Jesus is God

>> No other religion believes that

o Islam – Jesus is not god, didn't die on the cross, wasn't resurrected

o Judaism – Jesus is not Messiah/God

o Hinduism – universe is god, so Jesus is not God

>> So if we determine that Christianity is true through examination of the evidence, then anything that teaches the opposite is false

o Therefore all other religions are false

>> How do we decide if Christianity is true? - examine the evidence

Law of noncontradiction – law of opposites

- 2 things that teach opposites cannot both be true at same time and same sense

JOSEPH SOLD	
Scripture verses	Gen 37
High level key topic	When you think you are alone, you can trust that God is with you

SCRIPTURAL LESSON NARRATIVE

This month we focus on trust. Trust is when you put your belief in someone you can depend upon. Often times in life we cannot explain or understand why things happen in our lives. It is confusing and we usually want to try to take control of all the circumstances ourselves. Yes, we should do what we can but first we should pray and ask God to guide us. Then He will guide our steps. When things are all wrong, problems and suffering happen. Instead of trying to understand why these things would happen and what to do about it, pray and turn it over to God. Say, "Lord, I don't know why this has to be, but I trust you and will continue to have faith that you will do what is best. Guide me to do what you want of me." Then don't worry about it anymore and focus on the next thing you think you need to do. Leave the rest to God.

Our scripture is about the story of Joseph because he is one of the best examples of trust in the Bible. It explains how the Israelites ended up as slaves in Egypt eventually. Today we will just look at the beginning of the story. Remember last week we had the lesson about Abraham and his son Isaac, how God asked him to sacrifice him as a test of faith, but then stopped him before it happened. And God promised Abraham, then Isaac, that all their descendants would form all nations of the earth. Isaac grew up to have two sons, Jacob and Esau. Jacob was the favored son. When Jacob grew very old he had his last son Joseph. Sometimes when a parent has a child in old age, they favor them and spoil them. That was what Abraham did with Isaac and now it happens with Jacob and his son Joseph.

Joseph is made responsible, even though the youngest brother, to track and report on his brothers' activities tending the flocks for his father. This makes the other brothers jealous. Jacob gives a special coat of many colors to Joseph and again the brothers are jealous. Then Joseph has a dream and tells his brothers that one day they will all bow down to him and he will rule over them. This angers them and they begin to plot against him.

One day as Joseph travels to find his brothers tending flock and report about their activities they see him coming and plot to kill him. They throw him in a pit and plan to leave him there. The oldest brother Reuben tries to save him but the other brothers win out. But because he is their brother, they change their mind and sell him to a trading caravan that comes by on the way to Egypt and receive 20 pieces of silver. The caravan then sells him to Potiphar, the captain of the guard for Pharaoh. Joseph never loses his faith in God through this ordeal and trusts that God has a plan for him.

DOES GOD EXIST?
- PART 1

Now that we know there is such a thing as truth, that truth is undeniable, and anything opposite of the truth is false, we begin to examine the evidence to show Christianity is true. First, we have to understand if God really exists. We can look at the evidence from science and philosophy for this without even using the Bible, although Gen 1:1 explains it also.

How do we know God exists? Because He is the most likely cause for the creation of the universe. Until 25 years ago, most scientists thought the universe was eternal; in other words that it always existed. But they made some discoveries that showed it actually had a beginning. Understand that this created a big problem for scientists who didn't believe in God because if the universe had a beginning, what caused it? The law of causality in science is one of the most accepted there is. Anything that begins to exist must have a cause. There is a cause and effect for every event or activity that takes place.

They learned from Einstein's theory of relativity that before the universe began, there was no space, matter or time. It all started when the universe began. They call this event the Big Bang. But the Big Bang only describes that the universe began from nothing into something. It does not explain what caused the Big Bang. The Big Bang is actually a proof for God. Here are the statements that show it:

1. Whatever begins to exist has a cause

2. The universe began to exist

3. The universe must have a cause

But for something to be created out of nothing is a scientific impossibility. This is a mystery they cannot figure out unless they see that God created it as it says in Gen 1:1. Scientists believe that there is nothing beyond the material world. And the material world, or nature, was created. So whatever created the material world was beyond nature. Whatever created the universe was all powerful, incredibly intelligent, timeless, eternal, not made of matter, purposeful, and outside of the universe. Whether they call that God or not, it fits the description of characteristics of a Supreme Being that we call God.

Scientists have tried hard to explain this problem away. Mainly, some brilliant scientists have tried to say that nothing is actually something. They say the universe popped into existence from a quantum vacuum, which has energy and properties and fields. But that is something, not nothing. They have tried also to say that the universe starts and stops over and over again so it is actually not beginning but in a never ending cycle. That has no evidence and most scientists agree that the proof is that it had a beginning. So remember, the Big Bang does not disprove God. It points directly to God as the cause of the universe.

SEPTEMBER LESSONS

JOSEPH IN PRISON	
Scripture verses	Gen 40
High level key topic	When life doesn't make sense, you can trust God is with you

SCRIPTURAL LESSON NARRATIVE

This month we focus on trust. Trust is when you put your belief in someone you can depend upon.

We talked about how often times in life things go wrong or you have problems and you just can't understand why they are happening. You can pray for God to help you and to guide your steps but ask Him to take care of things and to help you get through them. Then relax and He will guide your steps. There will always be things you cannot control.

Last week we began the story of Joseph. Even though his brothers were jealous and sold him as a slave and he was sent to Egypt, Joseph still trusted that God would help him through his problems. In Egypt, he was sold to Potiphar, the captain of the guard of Pharaoh and a very important person.

Joseph became his servant and earned his favor. Potiphar saw Joseph pray and how he respected the Jewish God and how God blessed him so Potiphar began to like him more and trust him. He put him in charge of his entire household. After a time, Pharaoh's wife came to Joseph and had evil intentions to tempt him to be with her and betray himself. But he refused. Every day for a long time this happened. Finally, one day the wife grabbed Joseph and tried to kiss him but when he escaped her grasp to run away part of his garment was left behind. The wife was angry that he rejected her and she took the garment and went to her husband claiming that Joseph had attacked her. Potiphar was angry and threw Joseph in jail. Yet Joseph trusted God, prayed often and sang praise songs such that the prison warden began to trust him and the warden put Joseph in charge of all the prisoners.

One day two new prisoners came, the Pharaoh's cupbearer and baker. They were important positions but were put in prison for offending Pharaoh somehow. Joseph was made personal servant to attend to them. One night they both had dreams. Joseph said that God could help him interpret the dreams for them. The cupbearer's dream was that a vine had three branches of grapes so he squeezed the grapes into the cup and gave it to Pharaoh. Joseph said this meant in three days his head would be lifted up and restored to his position. Joseph asked that he remember him to Pharaoh and tell him he was innocent. Because it sounded like a good outcome, the baker told his dream. He had three baskets of baked goods on his head and birds were eating out of the top basket. Joseph said this meant in three days his head would be lifted up and he would be hanged.

Soon both the dreams that Joseph interpreted came true. But the cupbearer forgot Joseph and did not mention him to Pharaoh. The baker was hanged. Now Joseph was back in the same position as before. But he still trusted God.

Some day in your lives, if not already, things will happen you do not understand. Good things do sometimes happen to bad people, but also bad things happen to good people. Don't blame God. Pray and trust Him and ask Him to take control and guide your steps to help you through. Do you know why bad things happen in the world? (explain briefly the problem of evil and suffering.)

Pray that when something bad happens they will seek God, pray and turn it over to Him and trust Him to help them through.

DOES GOD EXIST?
– PART 2

So far we began our search for evidence to show Christianity is true by explaining that we can know truth because it is undeniable and corresponds to the facts. And if something teaches the opposite of a truth, then it is false. Then we began to study how we can know that God even exists. The first major piece of evidence is the creation of the universe. We know now that the universe is not eternal and had a beginning. Anything that begins to exist must have a cause. But whatever caused it to begin was outside the universe, not physical, timeless, all powerful and eternal. So the evidence for what created the universe points to God. Scientists have no satisfactory explanation otherwise and the evidence most likely shows God exists.

Today we will present a second argument for God's existence. We know now that the entire universe, galaxies, stars, solar systems, planets and everything that exists looks as if it is remarkably designed to support our life here on earth. Scientists are baffled by the fact that the universe is so remarkably ordered. Our life here on earth seems impossible and due to amazing chance and coincidence it makes it near impossible to understand unless it is designed the way it is.

In other words, it is beyond chance and probability that everything turned out perfectly to support our life one earth. It is virtually impossible it is by chance and much more likely that it was designed. In fact there are over 1000 physical requirements that had to happen exactly so in order for life to form on earth, and they have to remain constant or life cannot survive.

Here are some examples to think about:

1. Expansion rate of universe. If it expanded 1 millionth of a percentage faster or slower, galaxies would never have formed and been thrown apart, or gravity would have made them collapse.

2. Earth distance from the sun. 93 million miles. Takes 8 minutes for light to reach. What if only 7 or 9? We would either freeze or burn up and no life would be possible.

3. Oxygen is 21% of our atmosphere. In spite of all the plants and trees destroyed as cities were made and more were planted, the percentage is the same. If it were only 2% higher, fires would break out spontaneously or if it

were 2% less, we would suffocate and either way no life would be possible.

4. Also, if oxygen weighed just a small amount less and poison gases such as chlorine and ammonia weighed slightly more, oxygen would not stay in our atmosphere and the poison gases would kill us instead of floating out of the atmosphere.

5. H_2O is the only molecule that has three states where the most solid state is the lightest. If the most solid state was the heaviest, ice would sink and all living things in the sea would be destroyed and life as we know it would be destroyed.

6. The spin rate of the earth if slower or faster would cause turbulent weather and we could not survive.

7. The existence of the moon and its distance from us helps control the tides of the oceans or they might sweep across the land and flood all civilization out.

8. Our atmosphere allows a certain amount of radiation and heat but if it were more or less we could not survive.

9. Jupiter's location. It is like a vacuum cleaner and catches stray asteroids and meteors and protects us from collisions.

10. Volcanoes and earthquakes. If there were more or less the earth would either be destroyed or lack key nitrogen deposits for life to survive.

These are just a few. Scientists are befuddled as to how to explain. Some merely say it "appears" the universe is perfectly ordered and designed. Some have become believers in God because of it. Some invented the theory of the multiverse with no evidence whatsoever. As Christians we know it is because designed everything for human life on earth.

PHARAOH'S DREAM	
Scripture verses	Gen 41
High level key topic	When the pressure is on, you can trust God is with you

SCRIPTURAL LESSON NARRATIVE

This month we focus on trust. Trust is when you put your belief in someone you can depend upon.

We've been studying the story of Joseph and how he had amazing trust in God through all his difficulties. Last week when we ended, Joseph was in prison. Remember his jealous brothers had sold him into slavery and he went to work for Potiphar, the captain of the guard in Egypt for Pharaoh. He ended up in charge of the whole household but was falsely accused of attacking Pharaoh's wife and thrown in prison. He ended up in charge of all the prisoners. There he helped the cupbearer and baker interpret their dreams when Pharaoh also threw them in prison. The cupbearer was restored to his position but the baker was hanged as Joseph predicted. But the cupbearer forgot to tell Pharaoh that Joseph helped him.

For two years Joseph remained in prison. Then Pharaoh had a disturbing dream. The dreams we have mentioned a few times are really visions, where sometimes God chooses to speak to people in their dream. Sometimes the people didn't understand the dreams. Pharaoh saw first 7 fat cows by the Nile, then 7 ugly skinny cows there, and then the skinny cows ate the fat ones but still remained ugly and skinny. Then he saw 7 grains of wheat in the sunlight, and then 7 thin scorched ones that took over the 7 good ones but still remained scorched. He called for his magicians and they didn't know what it meant. Suddenly the cupbearer remembered Joseph and told Pharaoh how he interpreted his dreams. So Pharaoh called for Joseph and told him the dream. Imagine the pressure he was under. If he could not explain the dream or even if Pharaoh did not like the dream, he would probably be killed.

Joseph said he could not explain it but God could explain it through him. He said the 7 cows and 7 grains of wheat were years. There would be 7 good years and then 7 bad years of terrible famine. He told Pharaoh someone should arrange 1/5 of all the food to be stored each year of the 7 good years. Then when the famine came there would be enough for everyone. Pharaoh decided to put Joseph in charge of this program. He became 2nd in charge of all Egypt and even gave him his ring to wear and a wife. During the good years, Joseph went from city to city arranging the storage of the harvest. When the famine came, it was beyond terrible. But the storage was sufficient to feed the people. Even other countries came to buy food it was so bad. Joseph had two children by his new wife and they were named in honor of God and Joseph was given a new name in honor of God. When the pressure is on you can trust God to help you through.

APOLOGETICS LESSON (DEFENDING CHRISTIANITY)

DOES GOD EXIST?
– PART 3

So far we began our search for evidence to show Christianity is true by explaining that we can know truth because it is undeniable and corresponds to the facts. And if something teaches the opposite of a truth, then it is false. Then we began to study how we can know that God exists. The first major piece of evidence is the creation of the universe. We know now that the universe is not eternal and had a beginning. Anything that begins to exist must have a cause. But whatever caused it to begin was outside the universe, not physical, timeless, all powerful and eternal. So the evidence for what created the universe points to God. Scientists have no satisfactory explanation otherwise and the evidence most likely shows that God exists.

Last week we showed that the universe seems to be perfectly designed just to support life on earth. The vastness and laws of nature are just so perfectly arranged that life can exist and continue. If the laws of nature or our natural world were even the slightest different, life could not exist. We talked about our distance from the sun, and the moon, the rotation of the earth, the percentage of oxygen in the air. Some scientists are so convinced the universe looks designed perfectly that they have come to believe in God or at least admit everything looks like it was intelligently designed. The possibility that random chance set everything up has been ruled out mathematically. Show 70 rolls of dice video.

Today, we are going to explain how all living things appear to be designed. Show living cell video from Illustra Media CD.

Every living thing: plants, animals, mammals, fish, birds, humans has DNA, an amazing amount of information that actually controls the messages that tell cells how to do everything needed to grow and survive. But we know that information always comes from an intelligent source. It cannot randomly come together and form a message on the beach like, "John loves Mary." If you saw that, you would know some intelligent force caused it. Such is every living thing. If it is not random and yet it is intelligent, what caused it? An Intelligent Designer; God.

A single living cell has enough information comparable to 1000 volumes of encyclopedias. Not just random characters and words, but coded messages, like an instruction manual. It contains the instructions to make proteins which build all the different types of cells, there are error correcting chemicals, a storage system, transportation system, communications system, even a waste removal system. Essentially it is like a little city.

Even if one believes evolution is true, it cannot explain how life began. The best explanation scientists who are not believers have now is 'panspermia', in other words life came from somewhere else in the universe and arrived here. But that does not solve the problem of where that life came from even if it was true.

Scientists who are not believers are frustrated by all this incredible evidence. But they only admit it in private unless they are a believer. Otherwise if they announce it in public, they may lose their jobs at the universities, funding for their projects, and get kicked out of the National Academy of Science. It is now like a big political cover up. They don't want anyone to know they cannot really explain what caused the universe, how to explain the universe is perfectly designed for life, and how life began – unless they admit it is most likely a Supreme Being, all intelligent and all powerful, outside the universe, eternal and timeless: what Christians call God.

MOSES	
Scripture verses	Exodus 2:1-10
High level key topic	You can do what you should even when you don't know what will happen next.

SCRIPTURAL LESSON NARRATIVE

Last month we discussed trust and the story of Joseph and how what his brothers meant for evil, God meant for good. This month we focus on courage. Courage is when you may have fear but you are brave enough to do the right thing anyway. Let's review the story of Moses.

Remember, when we ended the story of Joseph, he had Jacob and all his brothers and their families move to Egypt where he could care for them. There were about 70 in the family. Over many years, the family grew rapidly and after Joseph and his brothers and father were gone, there was a new Pharaoh who did not care about the old promises given to Joseph to take care of the family. By this time the Israelites had expanded so rapidly that the new Pharaoh was worried because there were so many of them. He decided to put them into slavery to control them. They built many great cities and pyramids for him. But they had many more children and expanded even more rapidly than before. He worried that if an outside army came to conquer, the Israelite slaves might join them and revolt against him. So he told the birth nurses to kill any baby boys that were born to stop the population from expanding. But the birth nurses believed in God and ignored his command. Finally, Pharaoh ordered all the Israelites to throw any newborn babies into the Nile to be destroyed.

One Israelite family had a beautiful baby boy and she hid him for 3 months instead of following the order. But from fear he would be discovered, one day she made a basket and sealed it with tar and put the baby into it and placed it among the reeds in the Nile. She had to have great courage to give up her baby and somehow trust that God would take care of it for her. The baby's sister watched over the baby to see what would happen.

Later Pharaoh's daughter was bathing in the Nile and saw the basket and commanded her servants to get it for her. When she saw there was a baby boy, she knew he was an Israelite but lovd him anyway. At that time the baby's sister came up to her and asked if she wanted her to get someone to help her nurse the baby and raise it. She said yes and ironically the sister went to get her mother, the baby's actual mother, and Pharaoh's daughter paid the mother to nurse the baby until old enough for her to bring him back to the palace. What an amazing story! Once again, God had a greater plan to bring good out of evil.

When you are in a situation where you have fear, pause and say a prayer and ask God for strength and bravery to do the right thing. Maybe you see someone bullying someone at your school, or making fun of a child who is handicapped or has special needs. Whatever it may be, courage is when you have fear but are brave enough to do the right thing anyway.

DOES GOD EXIST?
– PART 4 THE MORAL LAW

So far we have covered 3 main lines of evidence that God exists

1. Creation of the universe from nothing

   a. Better explanation than science

2. Intelligent design of the universe to support life

   a. Virtually impossible odds it all happened from chance

3. Creation of first life

   a. Virtually impossible odds it all happened from chance

   b. All life contains vast amounts of information that must come from an intelligent Source

Today I want to explain another evidence for God. We call it the Moral law. Moral is a word meaning the principles of right and wrong. So how is this evidence for God?

Well, it is an important issue to determine where our morals come from. How do we determine what is right and wrong? Is it your opinion, or your neighbor's, each of us, the government, or your parents? Who decides? If there is no set of rules that determine for all of society and even the world what is right and wrong, then each may choose something different and this can turn into constant fighting and arguing, and wars. We have that throughout history and even now.

How do we know Hitler was bad unless there is some set of rules or laws that we all accept? Otherwise we have no reason to say what he did was wrong if we don't have a standard.

If there are any acts in the world that everyone agrees are bad, then there must be some moral law that causes us to feel and believe that. For example, does anyone agree that helping people is bad, or that bad is good, or torturing babies for fun is good? If we all agree those are wrong then there are at least a couple of moral laws that we seem to all agree on for some reason. But where does that idea that we ought to do this or ought not to do that come from that seems to be inside of us? It is because God has written these Moral Laws on our hearts. Some may still not follow them, but they know they are doing wrong. Some people might call this our conscience. We are calling it also our Moral Law. Here is the formal argument:

1. All laws have a law giver

2. There is a moral law

3. So there is a moral law giver.

We all have it in our hearts that love is better than hate, good is better than bad; murder is bad, and hundreds of other ideas. These are not just for individuals but everyone and all nations.

Sometimes all the moral laws may not be easy to recognize, but they are there for everyone. And some may try to deny it because they do not want to admit that God exists.

Let's look at it more simply. Does everyone agree that evil exists in the world? I think so. But many say that evil proves God does not exist or He would destroy it. But actually it is just the opposite. If there is evil, it is a proof for God. If we can agree that there is an absolute standard of good, then this proves God exists because it comes from outside of ourselves yet we all have this idea of how to know if something is good or evil. Sometimes the in between parts get fuzzy and require more study and thought but how do you recognize that something is evil unless there is an all good standard to compare it to. Otherwise it is just one opinion against another.

ADAM AND EVE CHOSE

Scripture verses	Genesis 3
High level key topic	We have the freedom to choose. Choose wisely.

SCRIPTURAL LESSON NARRATIVE

Today's lesson details the fall of man; the beginning of sin. The setting is the Garden of Eden where Adam and Eve were warned by God not to eat from the tree of the knowledge of good and evil. But Eve is deceived by the serpent and then tempts Adam to eat from the tree also. God is forced to discipline them. Eve and all women to follow will receive more pain during labor and giving birth. And her offspring will continuously have to fight against evil. Adam and all men will have to work the land for food.

The bad choices they both made led to their physical death. Actually it was merciful on God's part so that they would not live forever and endure sin and evil. But they would still live spiritually.

They disobeyed God and did what they wanted to do instead of what God wanted. They were free to make that choice but it had consequences. We too will suffer consequences from our sins. But when we pray to God and ask forgiveness He heals us and we are no longer separated from His love.

A sin is anything you think, say or do that displeases God. Adam and Even tried to hide their sin from God but they could not. Nor can you. Pray to God and ask Him to reveal your sins to you so you can pray for forgiveness. Don't try to hide them or ignore them because it will only make things worse. Also pray and ask God to give you the strength to accept responsibility when you do wrong.

WHY DOES GOD GIVE US FREE WILL AND THEREFORE CREATE THE POSSIBILITY FOR SIN?

God could have created us all so there was no possibility of sin. He could have forced us to love Him and forced us to always do right. So why did He not do that instead?

Well, first, forced love is a contradiction. It is not love at all. It is a form of abuse when you make someone do what you want even if they do not wish to. What benefit would God create by having billions of people who were forced to love Him like slaves? Would that glorify His name? No. It would only make Him a dictator and slave master of sorts. And it would create a world of people with no will power of their own.

With no freedom of choice, we cannot begin to grow our character and become better people because there is never a mistake made and therefore no appreciation for consequences or for taking responsibility. There is no path for moral growth at all.

But with free will, we all have the opportunity to learn from our mistakes. That can make us better people. It can make us appreciate the benefits of good choices and the disadvantages of bad choices. As we become better at it during our lives, we are actually preparing ourselves in the way that God wants for our life after death. We don't know exactly what things will be like in heaven, but the Bible is clear that our life here on earth is meant to prepare us to be ready for what we will experience in heaven.

their sin from God but they could not. Nor can you. Pray to God and ask Him to reveal your sins to you so you can pray for forgiveness. Don't try to hide them or ignore them because it will only make things worse. Also pray and ask God to give you the strength to accept responsibility when you do wrong.

OCTOBER LESSONS

MOSES IS CALLED	
Scripture verses	Exodus 3-12
High level key topic	You can do what you should even when you don't feel ready

SCRIPTURAL LESSON NARRATIVE

Courage is when you may have fear but you are brave enough to do the right thing anyway. In the beginning of the story of Moses, Pharaoh was very worried that there were so many Israelites and they might rebel and overturn his kingdom. He put them into slavery and when that didn't work, he called for the killing of all male infants. Moses' mother hid him for 3 months then trusted God and put him in a basket in the Nile. Pharaoh's daughter picked him up and Moses' sister went to get someone to nurse the baby for Pharaoh's daughter until he was old enough to be in the palace on his own. Ironically, the nurse turned out to be Moses' real mother and they even paid her to nurse him. Her courage was rewarded.

Later when Moses grew up, he was tending sheep and saw a burning bush that was not being consumed. God spoke to Him and told Him it was time to bring the Israelites out of slavery and that he selected Moses to do it. Moses had fear and many objections and actually begged God to send someone else. He had a stuttering problem and was afraid to speak with Pharaoh directly. God said, "Who made the human mouth?" So God sent his brother Aaron along with him. Moses asked what name to call God and He responded, "I Am". He told Moses Pharaoh would not listen so many miracles would be done in front of him. His staff was able to turn into a snake and had power for other signs. And he put his hand inside his cloak and it became diseased until he repeated it. First Moses and Aaron spoke to the Israelites and used his staff to produce signs and they believed he would save them. Then he went to Pharaoh to demand that he release the people. Pharaoh refused and increased the workload on the slaves. The people complained to Moses and Moses questioned God about why He allowed this.

Moses went to Pharaoh and said God demanded the people's release. When he refused, Moses turned his staff into a snake but the court magicians somehow did the same and Pharaoh was not impressed. Pharaoh refused and Moses began a series of ten miracles done in the form of plagues to make Pharaoh and his people know who God was and to release the people. The plagues were: Nile turned to blood which caused the fish to die and people could not drink from it; but the magicians duplicated it and Pharaoh refused. Then the Lord sent frogs that swarmed the land. The magicians duplicated it but Pharaoh agreed to let them go the next day if Moses removed them, so God did. Then Pharaoh changed his mind and refused once everything was normal again. So God sent swarms of gnats, then flies and Pharaoh agreed to let the people go if Moses removed them. Once done, Pharaoh still refused. God sent a disease to all the livestock and they died, except for the Israelite livestock. Then God made boils appear on the Egyptians skin. Then God sent hail and Pharaoh agreed to let them go but then refused after the hail was gone. Then God sent locusts that ate all the crops and vegetation. The same thing happened. Then God sent darkness over the land for three days but the Israelites had light. Pharaoh refused and said he would kill Moses the next time he saw him.

Then God sent a plague to kill the firstborn of all the Egyptians, including Pharaoh's own son. God instructed Moses and the Israelites to prepare for the Passover. They took animals blood and painted it over their doorsteps so the angel of death would "pass over" their homes. A loud wailing went up throughout Egypt and Pharaoh told Moses to leave with the people once his son was killed. The Egyptians even gave their gold and valuables to the Israelites to get rid of them. After 430 years in slavery to Egypt, they left.

Keep in mind our lesson. Although Moses had many fears and excuses and objections, he finally found enough courage to do what God asked him. When you have fear in your life or an important decision, pray first and ask for God's guidance, then be confident He is with you when you take your next steps.

IS THE BIBLE RELIABLE?
– PART 1

So far we have covered 4 main lines of evidence that God exists

1. Creation of the universe – something came from nothing

2. Creation of life – nonliving chemicals became living

3. Intelligent design – universe designed to support life on earth

4. Moral law – if there is evil, God exists because otherwise how do you recognize it as evil without an all perfect standard of goodness to compare

Today, we are starting a new line of evidence – can we trust the bible? Is it reliable? This is a critical issue because so much of Christianity is based on the bible.

First, let's look at a few serious challenges that we need to deal with. Critics and nonbelievers and skeptics claim:

• The Bible is myth and legends and stories which are just like legends, like fairy tales

• The Bible has many errors

• The Bible was written several hundred years after Jesus so you can't trust what it says

• The Bible is copies of copies of copies so you cannot trust it

• It is full of miracles and miracles are not possible

To answer these questions, please be aware that some of these are difficult questions. But when we are finished with our explanations, you will see that we can trust the Bible as the inspired word of God.

First, we must understand that it is true that we have no originals of the Bible, or for any of the individual books. This is not unusual as there are no ancient manuscripts that survive from that time. However, we have good reason to be confident about all the copies we have since the time of Jesus. Here's why.

Manuscript copies – 5400 NT Greek copies and 24,000 in Latin and other languages.

• A dozen manuscripts from the second century

• 64 from the third century

- **48 from the 4th century**

- **Totaling 124 within 300 yrs.**

- **Oldest is called John Ryland fragment – 4 verses from John**

    o **Circa AD 110-130**

- **Think of it like a puzzle and put it together**

Compared to other ancient manuscripts, there are only a couple hundred available from works like Plato and the Odyssey and none are originals. You can trust we have enough copies to compare for accuracy and to reconstruct what the originals said.

JOSHUA AND CALEB

Scripture verses	Numbers 13-14
High level key topic	You can do what you should even when others are afraid

SCRIPTURAL LESSON NARRATIVE

This month we focus on courage. Courage is when you may have fear but you are brave enough to do the right thing anyway. We reviewed the story of Moses. He was saved from death in a basket on the Nile and raised in Pharaoh's palace. Later he led his people out of slavery in Egypt and parted the Red Sea miraculously with God's help. Now they are about to come upon their destination – the Promised Land, Canaan.

Moses sends out 12 spies to survey the land they are supposed to conquer and take over. It is fertile and fruitful. But the cities have high walls and are fortified and strong, and the people are very tall, some like giants. All the spies become fearful except for Joshua and Caleb. After 40 days they return to report to Moses. They tell him the land is rich and wonderful but the cities and people are strong and tall and fortified and they cannot defeat them. But Joshua and Caleb stand up and insist that they can defeat them because it is what God has called them to do. All the Israelites become scared and begin to complain and rebel against Moses, and say that they want a new leader who will take them back to Egypt. Moses and Aaron pray to the Lord and He says that the spies will be destroyed for their rebellion, except Joshua and Caleb, and that as punishment for disobeying God all the people will wander in the wilderness for 40 years before he allows them to take over the land. Suddenly the people realize they are wrong and decide to attack the Canaanites after all. But Moses tells them not to because now God has given them a different command. But they don't listen and instead are defeated by the Canaanites.

Today's lesson shows us we can have courage even when others are afraid. We can follow God's commands even though we have fear. The lesson may be hard to relate to in today's times. You may not hear God giving you commands as He did in those times. But we have His commands written for us in the Bible so we know how to live our lives. Follow the teachings of the bible and of Jesus and you will know how to live your life. When trouble finds you, pray and ask God for guidance and help. Then be confident that He will help you through your difficulties. Be patient and always trust in God no matter what.

IS THE BIBLE RELIABLE?
– PART 2

So far we have covered 4 main lines of evidence that God exists

1. Creation of the universe – something came from nothing

2. Creation of life – nonliving chemicals became living

3. Intelligent design – universe designed to support life on earth

4. Moral law – if there is evil, God exists because otherwise how do you recognize it as evil without an all perfect standard of goodness to compare

Last time we began a new line of evidence – can we trust the bible? Is it reliable? This is a critical issue because so much of Christianity is based on the bible.

Even though we have no original of the Bible and no originals of any of the 66 books in the Bible we can still know we can trust it. We have Manuscript copies – 5400 Greek copies and 24,000 in Latin and other languages.

• A dozen manuscripts from the second century

• 64 from the third century

• 48 from the 4th century

• Totaling 124 within 300 yrs.

• Oldest is called John Ryland fragment – 4 verses from John

   o Circa AD 110-130

• Think of it like a puzzle and put it together

When you compare all the copies over several hundred years, you are able to discover what the originals said and that they all compare with 95% accuracy or better. This is unheard of for any ancient manuscripts.

And compared to other ancient manuscripts, there are only a couple hundred available from works like Plato, Alexander the Great and the Odyssey and none are originals.

Today we add one more piece of evidence that shows we can trust the Bible – early eyewitness testimony.

- It has been said by a legal scholar that the gospels alone are such historically accurate documents that the authors could testify in a court of law and be accepted.

- All the 9 authors of the NT were either direct eyewitnesses of the events they described or they were reporters who interviewed the people who saw the events such as Jesus and all the miracles and even the resurrection.

Here are some key facts that show early testimony and writing of the NT:

1. Paul killed in late AD 60's

   a. So he had to write all his works before then - epistles

2. James killed in AD 63 – according to a Jewish historian

   a. This is Jesus' brother yet it is not mentioned in the NT

3. Acts written by AD 62

   a. So Luke was earlier because Acts mentions it

4. But Mark is known to be earlier than that

5. And Matthew follows

6. 1 Cor., written by AD 55 – accepted by even the most critical scholars

7. Temple destroyed in AD 70 but no mention

   a. The temple was their sacred daily place of worship for 3000 years

   i. It's destruction would certainly be mentioned if it had happened yet

   b. Would you write a book about Lincoln or JFK and not mention their assassinations?

   c. But their documents still talk about the temple and events that happen in and around it

   d. If it was not mentioned, it means it had not happened yet

Some people insist this is not early enough but it is earlier by far than any ancient book.

So the Bible is not myth and legend. It was written very close to the time of the events.

Remember that 98% of the population could not read or write. They memorized everything and passed it on that way. But the NT authors could read and write. Remember that there were no copiers or printing presses at that time.

Remember that after Jesus' resurrection, Christians were hunted down and killed so they were on the run and there was little time to write. Yet they were still written within 30 years of the resurrection.

These are some of the proofs that help us know the Bible is accurate and early. But how do we know it is actually true? Next time.

BATTLE OF JERICHO

Scripture verses	Joshua 5:13-6:27
High level key topic	You can do what you should because God is with you.

SCRIPTURAL LESSON NARRATIVE

This month we focus on courage. Courage is when you may have fear but you are brave enough to do the right thing anyway.

Moses and the Israelites wandered in the desert for 40 years because of their disobedience when God told them to fight the Canaanites. They became scared and the spies convinced them they could not win. But Joshua and Caleb were two loyal and faithful spies. The other spies were killed and when the people too late realized they should obey, they tried to fight the Canaanites and were defeated. God had already told them not to at that time. So after 40 years now they are ready to take over Canaan again and the major city of Jericho.

By now, Moses had died and Joshua was the new leader; a military man. They have Jericho surrounded but it is heavily fortified with a huge wall around it. Joshua had spent two spies to scout the city and they were helped by a woman named Rahab who hid them inside the walls through a secret entrance and told them all about how the city was protected.

Now Joshua encounters a man who calls himself the commander of the Lord's army. This is actually an appearance of the Angel of the Lord/Jesus as occurs several times in the OT. This is Jesus before he was born of Mary and appears here in the form of a military man. Joshua bows to him which he would only do for worship of God. Then God tells Joshua how to defeat the city. He will march with the whole army around the city once a day for six days with priests and the Ark of the Covenant in front. Then on the seventh day they circle the city seven times and at the end they blow the trumpets and shout and the walls fall. Then they enter and capture the city but save Rahab and her family because they helped. This is no coincidence as Rahab is an ancestor of Joseph, who marries Mary and gives birth to Jesus. So the line of Jesus legally on Joseph's side of the family comes from Rahab who later has a descendant who fathers Boaz, who marries Ruth, who has a descendant Jesse, who is the father of King David, and so on. If Rahab had been killed during the battle, that line of descendants would not have produced Joseph. It's amazing how God works!

The key message today is that we can have courage to do what is right because God is with us. Never forget that. When you have difficulties in your life, pray to God for guidance and turn your troubles over to Him, then He will guide your next steps and you can find peace with the knowledge that He is in control.

IS THE BIBLE RELIABLE?
- PART 3

So far we have covered 4 main lines of evidence that God exists

1. Creation of the universe – something came from nothing

2. Creation of life – nonliving chemicals became living

3. Intelligent design – universe designed to support life on earth

4. Moral law – if there is evil, God exists because otherwise how do you recognize it as evil without an all perfect standard of goodness to compare

5. The Bible is reliable

   a. 5700 copies still in existence that compare accurately to 95% or better

   b. 124 partial or full copies within 300 years of Jesus (more by far than any ancient document)

   c. Early scripture in the NT shows some books were recorded within 30 years of the resurrection and all the NT was written before AD 70 because that is when Jerusalem and the temple were destroyed, but there is no mention of it in the NT. That is because it had not yet happened.

      i. Compared to other ancient manuscripts, there are only a couple hundred available from works like Plato, Alexander the Great and the Odyssey and none are originals and all written 600-1500 years after their deaths.

      ii. Remember that 98% of the population could not read or write. They memorized everything and passed it on that way. But the NT authors could read and write. Remember that there were no copiers or printing presses at that time and Christians were on the run from Roman executioners and had little time or means to record writings and copy them over and over.

Today we add the final piece of evidence. How do we know what the writers wrote was actually true?

1. The 9 authors of the NT were all either eyewitnesses of the events when they happened or they interviewed the eyewitnesses while they were still alive (i.e. Luke, who wrote Luke and Acts)

   a. Also, even the most critical bible scholars (Bart Ehrman) agrees that the Bible is historically accurate but he just doesn't believe in miracles so he thinks that part was exaggerated

2. Embarrassing details

    a. If someone was writing a story about the resurrection or miracles, would they not write it in a way to prevent their own embarrassment of any events?

        i. The disciples often were dull and did not understand what Jesus said and meant

        ii. The disciples didn't understand Jesus was God until close to the crucifixion and resurrection

        iii. They all ran when Jesus was arrested

        iv. Except for John and the women, none were at the crucifixion

        v. The leader of the disciples, Peter, denied Him 3 times

        vi. Jesus was said to be crazy by His family at one time

        vii. James, his own brother, did not believe in him until the resurrection

        viii. Many disciples deserted him after the last supper

        ix. Jesus is accused of being demon-possessed by religious leaders

        x. Jesus, although God, is described as going through tremendous pain and suffering

        xi. The women were first witnesses to the resurrected Jesus (but female testimony not valid in a court of law)

        xii. Straightforward descriptions of miracles and resurrection and raising the dead with no exaggeration or emphasis

The only explanation for these strange details is that they were true. If they were trying to persuade people of lies they would certainly leave them out because they did not help their argument to persuade anyone that Jesus was God and resurrected.

These are some of the proofs that help us know the Bible is accurate and early. Believe it because it is true.

READ THE WORD

Scripture verses	Nehemiah 8:1-12
High level key topic	God provided His word so we would know what He expects from us. Read it.

SCRIPTURAL LESSON NARRATIVE

This month we are discussing God's Word, the Bible. Today we emphasize the importance of reading the Word each day. How many of you read from the Bible regularly? How often? Which parts? Do you understand it? What questions do you have about it? Do you seek answers for your questions from your parents? All these are critical to becoming a more mature Christian and truly learning the meaning of the Bible and understanding God's teachings and commands to us.

From the OT, today's lesson is about how the people of Israel listened to their priest, Ezra, as he read the book of law to them from daybreak to noon. He stood on a very tall wooden platform with the scripture open and all the people stood. Beside Ezra were many of the other local religious leaders to support him. As he read the book of law from Moses, the people began to weep, understanding how they had forgotten God's word and had not kept it, often worshipping other Gods and not following God's commandments. It became a sacred day for them and Ezra prayed for all of them to receive God's blessings and forgiveness.

When we acknowledge to God that we have done wrong, He is quick to forgive. So we should behave accordingly in our lives each day. None of us is free from sin. But when we do and think and say things each day that we should not, this displeases God. That is what we call sin. So each night, read from the Bible perhaps one chapter, then pray and ask God's forgiveness for your sins from the day and He will forgive them and bless you. Get into this habit and you will find God's peace and grow as a Christian.

HOW DO WE KNOW THE BIBLE IS TRUE?

Beyond believing in Christianity and that the Bible is true, do we have good evidence to show that it is actually true, and not just a group of interesting stories that many critics and nonbelievers say were all made up?

Yes, in fact we have great evidence to show the Bible is true. Only the Bible, of all the world's religious scriptures, is a historical record that corresponds to history and was written by eyewitnesses of key events, or written by reporters who interviewed eyewitnesses. Let's just name a few key reasons to support our confidence that the Bible is true.

1. Not a myth or legend. Scholars say it takes at least two generations for stories to become myths and legends. The Bible was written within the same generation of Jesus. The earliest actual piece of a manuscript from the book of John that is still saved, called the John Ryland fragment, is dated around 110 AD. But we know from other scripture that some of the books of the NT were written as early as 20-30 years after Jesus' death and resurrection.

2. Many corresponding manuscript copies. For the NT alone, there are over 5700 Greek copies in existence of manuscripts from the NT. No ancient book has anything similar or even close yet we accept things from other ancient books as fact, such as Homer and the Ilyad, works of literature from a similar era. Comparing all 5700 manuscripts, the only errors found are copying errors (typos) and none have anything to do with any important key principles from the scripture. So we can be assured that there is corresponding truth among all the copies.

3. Written by eyewitnesses. The 9 authors of the NT were all either eyewitnesses to the events of Jesus' death and resurrection, or in His presence at some time, or were reporters who interviewed eyewitnesses. Eyewitness testimony is critical today to be valid in a court of law. Other religions' scriptures are not historical records by eyewitnesses but rather stories, legends or visions that were recorded with no evidence of their truth.

So, we can be very sure that the Bible is in fact a record of history and we can believe it. No challenges have ever been successful to prove that the Bible is not true.

NOVEMBER LESSONS

November obviously includes the Thanksgiving holiday and in some churches they may forego Sunday school and opt for a combined worship service, anticipating scarce attendance. Also, the same happens in December. In our church there are two weeks at least in December with no Sunday school class and a combined worship service. It always bothered me that we were unable to teach key messages like the Christmas story and birth of Jesus, all the prophecies about him, and so forth. So we decided to cover those topics early. As a result, through November and December we cover a lot more about Jesus and even the resurrection and the Christmas story.

SAMUEL SELECTS DAVID	
Scripture verses	1 Samuel 16:1-13
High level key topic	Honor others by giving them a chance

SCRIPTURAL LESSON NARRATIVE

This month we focus on honor. Honor is letting someone know you see how valuable they really are. Are the best looking, most powerful, wealthy and successful people the ones we should honor because they have the most? Not necessarily. God asks us not to look at people from the outside but rather the inside. God judges value by a person's heart. What they desire and their spiritual qualities. Throughout the Bible God uses and selects people to fulfill purposes that you would never choose yourself probably. In fact it is often just the opposite. Moses had a severe speaking impediment yet he was chosen to convince Pharaoh to let the Israelites go. Jesus' first disciples were merely fishermen, not religious leaders. Jesus Himself was born in humble circumstances in a stable or cave and was a carpenter in his early life.

So we should look at people in the same way. Sometimes the ones who have the most value on the inside are the ones who look like they have the least value on the outside. So it is with our lesson today, as the prophet Samuel is told by the Lord to select a new King. The prior King, Saul, was tall and strong and a mighty warrior. The people wanted him to be their king. But he failed them and continued to be selfish and made bad decisions, sometimes evil ones. So God decided to lift up a new King and appoint the one He wanted this time to show the people the difference and help them learn what to value in someone.

As our story begins, God tells the prophet Samuel to go to the town of Bethlehem and find Jesse, who has 7 sons and that He will instruct Samuel which one to appoint as the next King. The word used is actually anoint, which means to dedicate and the custom was to use oil and rub it over the person's head. But Samuel is afraid that if he follows God's command that King Saul will find out what he is doing and have him killed. So God has Samuel take a young cow as a sacrifice and to tell the people that is his purpose for being there. Some might think that God has caused Samuel to lie and deceive by doing so. But in this case, it is merely leaving out part of the truth in order to protect Samuel who has a greater purpose to fulfill. And he indeed does do the sacrifice so it is not a lie and deception. Sometimes in your own lives you may need to make decisions that make you a little uncomfortable when perhaps you have to choose from two evils or two bad choices. First pray about it and make your decision based on the greater command or expectation from God that you know is better. Some might say selection of a political leader is such a choice.

When Samuel arrives, he makes his sacrifice and invites Jesse and his sons to attend. Then afterwards, privately, Samuel looks at each of the sons of Jesse. But God rejects all of them, telling Samuel He judges what is in a man's heart, not what they look like from the outside. Finally, the youngest son, David, arrives from tending the sheep and Samuel anoints him to be Israel's next king.

God saw that David's heart was good and that He would fulfill God's purposes. In your own lives, remember to treat even the poorest and least advantaged people with respect and honor, because that is how God sees people. When you begin to see others the way God sees them, you will be on the right path to understanding the command that we should love others the way we love ourselves. Perhaps next time you notice those in school who are overlooked and forgotten or looked down upon, and go over and say hi to them and give them a kind word or helping hand in some way. It is what God wants and will make you feel good about yourself and want to do more things that God wants you to do.

WHO WAS JESUS?

In our discussion of the evidence to show Christianity is true, we covered the evidence to show God exists and that the Bible is reliable and we can trust it.

We can know God exists because the scientific evidence points to God as creator of the universe, all life, and sustainer of all things. This is no vague claim but backed up by all the best evidence from science itself.

We know the Bible can be trusted because we have 5700 partial or full copies from the early centuries that compare to 95% accuracy. Any errors are accounted for from copying errors mainly. We also know the NT was written within 20-30 years of Jesus' resurrection because there is no mention of the temple destruction in AD 70. As the most important part of their lives for over 2000 years, certainly this would have been written about but since it was not it can only mean that the writings occurred before the destruction happened. We can know that what was written must be true because no writers trying to persuade others about the events they witnessed would write embarrassing and humiliating details about themselves and Jesus.

Today we advance to another important piece of evidence to defend the truth of Christianity. Who was/is the Person of Jesus?

Many today from other religions and critics and nonbelievers say he was a great prophet and teacher, but not God. This is a key separation and contradiction that distinguishes Christianity from all other religions. Christianity claims Jesus was God. If Jesus was God, then all other religions that deny it must be false because the law of opposites (noncontradiction) is a universal law of logic that states two things that teach opposites cannot both be true at the same time in the same sense. So, is Jesus God or not?

We can answer this question through the direct and indirect claims of Jesus and His disciples:

1. Claimed to be I Am/Yahweh which always meant God everywhere in the Bible

2. Claimed to be equal to the Father

3. Asked for prayer and worship in his name

4. Claimed to be the Messiah

5. Forgave sins

6. At his trial, John 8:58 "before Abraham was, I Am"

7. Said all authority was given him under heaven and earth

8. He was arrested for blasphemy, so the Jewish leaders thought He was claiming to be God

9. 30 times in the NT he is referred to as God

10. 9 times people bowed down to him and he never rebuked them

11. His disciples referred to Him as God many times

12. Produced miracles to prove His deity

Another way to look at it is to examine what a prophet means. If He was merely a prophet, then He was either a lunatic or false prophet because He continually predicted His own death and resurrection. But He also fulfilled that prediction so He was more than a great prophet; He was God.

An important comparison to note is with the claims of Islam. With the rapid growth and perverted terrorist tendencies of some Islam followers we must examine their claims that Jesus was a great prophet but not God. As we have shown, Jesus predicted His own death and resurrection. But they deny He died or was God. Yet they claim He was a great prophet. If He claimed to be God, showed Himself to be God, and fulfilled His death and resurrection claims, then He was God. Because a great prophet cannot make false predictions, their beliefs are false. Therefore their Holy Scripture, the Qur'an, is false, Islam is a false religion and the God they follow, Allah, is a false God. It can be no other way. But we cannot disrespect them and brag about our truth and their falsehood. It points up the need for us to reach out to them with love and understanding because what they believe will doom them.

Be confident that Jesus was God. It means everything to you and your salvation. If you have not already accepted Jesus as Lord and Savior, accept Jesus now if your heart is telling you to.

STEPPING IN	
Scripture verses	1 Samuel 25
High level key topic	Jesus stepped in to save us from our sins

SCRIPTURAL LESSON NARRATIVE

Before the prophet Samuel died, he had announced that David, a shepherd boy, would be the next king after King Saul. This angered Saul and after Samuel died, he spent many years hunting David to kill him and prevent him from being the next king. But God always spared him and protected him.

In today's lesson, David was with his army of 600 men and needed food for a feast they were planning. David and his men had camped in an area near a wealthy rancher named Nabal and had protected Nabal and his family from harm while they stayed on his land. David sent messengers for food but Nabal was evil and refused. This enraged David and he sent his whole army to wipe out Nabal and his ranch. But Nabal's wife Abigail was alerted to the problem. She gathered supplies and met David on his way to the ranch, apologized for her husband's behavior and offered the food. She made a beautiful speech that turned David's heart and made him realize he should not take vengeance into his own hands. She returned to her husband and the next day informed him. He was so angry he had a heart attack and died. Immediately when David found out, he sent his messengers to bring back Abigail as his wife.

It took great courage for a woman in those days to intervene between men and try to prevent the deaths of many. When you see a conflict in your home or among friends about to happen, can you have the courage to try and prevent harm amongst them? But you must be careful not to be harmed yourself in the midst of your attempts. Compromise is usually the key to settling a disagreement.

How do you handle disagreements and conflict in your life? First you must recognize it when it is happening. Then find a solution that is satisfactory for both parties. Compromise is an important skill in life for your dealings with your family, your friends, with others, in marriage, and at work. Just look at things from both points of view and find a solution that works for both sides.

DO CHRISTIANITY AND ISLAM WORSHIP THE SAME GOD?

We have talked a good deal about the idea that some people think all religions lead to heaven. Let's examine the two largest religions in the world and compare them to understand their beliefs about God.

Christianity is the world's largest religion with about 2.2 billion Christians. Islam is the second largest with about 1.6 billion Muslims. Many say that Islam is growing rapidly and will overtake Christianity someday as it is expanding rapidly in the Middle East and Europe. That is possible but it is often overlooked that Christianity is growing rapidly in Indonesia, the world's largest Muslim population, Africa and China. There may actually be more Christians in China than in America.

There are only 3 religions in the world that believe there is only one true God; Christianity, Islam and Judaism. Christianity believes in the Trinity and Islam believes in Allah. Can they be the same? No, because they contradict each other. Please see the chart below to see how the two religions view Jesus. He is the central point of comparison because Christians believe He is part of the Godhead.

CHRISTIANITY	ISLAM
Jesus is part of the trinity (Father, Son, Holy Ghost)	There is no trinity
Jesus claimed to be God	Jesus never claimed to be God
Jesus died on the cross	Jesus did not die on the cross
Jesus was resurrected	Jesus was not resurrected
Jesus asked for prayer in His name	Only prayer to Allah
Jesus said the only way to the Father was thru Him	Jesus was merely a prophet
Christians say the trinity is the Father, Son, and Holy Spirit	Islam says that Christians believe in the Father, Son and Mary
Christians believe God is personal	Islam believes you cannot have a personal relationship with God
Christians believe the original Bible scripture is without error	Islam believes the Bible is corrupt
Christians believe the Muslim scripture (Koran) is corrupt	Islam believes the Koran is the Word of Allah and has never been changed
The Christian God loves sinners but hates sin	Allah hates sinners

It seems pretty clear that there are very different views of God. When two things teach such opposites, both cannot be true. So it is clear that they cannot both be worshipping the same God if it were possible that both the Gods existed. However, because God is omnipotent, there can only be one God. A second God could not also be omnipotent by definition. So the two Gods cannot both be omnipotent and therefore only one can be true. Which is true? As we continue to see through our studies, Christianity has the evidence on its side to show that Christianity is true. Islam fails miserably with any tests for historical accuracy of scripture.

Be happy you are a Christian. But recognize that God asks us to share with others why we believe Christianity is true. Don't feel superior to a Muslim or someone who believes in another religion. Love them as Jesus loves us. Share the gospel with them in peace and love.

GOD DOESN'T PLAY FAVORITES

Scripture verses	Acts 10
High level key topic	God treats all people the same in Christ

SCRIPTURAL LESSON NARRATIVE

During Jesus' time, the Jewish thinking and teaching was to not associate with foreigners or outsiders. The Jews were considered to be God's chosen people and they thought that meant that only they were able to receive God's salvation and love. It was true that God had chosen to use them as His example for the entire world. But it was not true that only the Jews could receive God's grace and salvation. Today's lesson is about how that changed and they came to understand everyone was to be treated the same and was the same in God's eyes; even the Gentiles.

Cornelius was a Roman centurion who had a large household in Caesarea. Even though he was Roman, he worshiped the Jewish God. One day he had a vision from an angel that told him he was recognized for his deeds and worship of God and that he was to send messengers to seek a man named Simon Peter and bring him to the household to speak his words. Cornelius dispatched his men immediately.

A little later, Simon Peter also had a strange vision and saw a sheet filled with 4 footed animals, reptiles and birds, typically animals the Jews called unclean. The sheet was being lowered from heaven and the angel said "Get up, kill and eat". Peter said no because they were unclean. The vision occurred three times. Then Peter realized that the vision meant that God viewed everyone the same and treated everyone the same, not just the Jews, so that all could come to Christ. The angel told Peter that some men would be coming to see him and he should go with them because they had been sent by God. Just at that time the men appeared. They requested Peter go with them and speak his words to their master.

Peter travelled with them and upon arrival Cornelius bowed down and worshipped him. But Peter said he was just a man and had him get up. Cornelius asked Peter to tell them the words that God had given him for others. Peter then explained that Christ was brought into the world to save everyone, that he and the disciples had witnessed him in a resurrected body, and were told to spread the good news to everyone. As Peter was talking, the Holy Spirit descended upon, and into, everyone. The entire household of family and friends and servants was saved. Then Peter baptized them all.

Let us not forget as Christians, that although we know we have the real truth in Christ, others who are misguided, misled or who have not heard the good news about Jesus need to hear the words. It is part of all our responsibilities to reach out to others in love and help lead them to Christ. Pray now that God will give you the opportunity to reach others and the strength and words to help them find the truth about Christ.

WHAT ARE THE KEY BELIEFS IN OTHER RELIGIONS?

Below are some of the key comparisons of the main religions in the world.

BUDDHISM

Not really a belief in God or gods at all. It says we are all in a state of suffering because of our desires. But that we try to find an enlightened state of being (nirvana) through meditation and to try to eliminate our desires and become somewhat non-existent as an individual.

HINDUISM

Some 320 million gods and counting but 3 are considered most important – Brahma, Shiva and Vishnu. You go to a festival, bring back an idol, put it on your mantle or table, name it and start worshipping it as your personal god or household god. You can have multiple ones, each for a particular purpose, such as prosperity, health or battle. The gods and humans are subject to karma, the belief that we die and take on another life, over and over (incarnation). The new life is good or bad, depending upon whether we did good or bad in our previous life. This is how our morals and justice are delivered. Devotion to a particular god or sometimes yoga or meditation is how we spiritually stay connected and find our way and understanding. The goal is to achieve oneness with the god and to be non-existent as an individual.

ISLAM

There is only one god and that is Allah. Allah determines everything. There is no free will or choice. Their scripture is the Koran, written down over decades by followers of Mohammad, the final prophet according to them, who received god's words in visions. They believe humans are foolish sinners and need instruction through the Koran and must follow it. Final salvation is up to Allah and based on his determination alone. Muslims are taught to follow 5 pillars (prayer, giving to the poor, trip to Mecca to worship, daily recitations of scripture, and fasting). Future salvation, if earned based on having more good works than bad, is in a paradise where we receive all the pleasures we lacked on earth. Those who do not believe in Islam will be in hell.

JUDAISM

Typically thought of as what the Jews believe. But being Jewish merely means born of a Jewish mother. Your religion could be anything. Judaism teaches the Old Testament first 5 books as a way of life (Torah). Reformed

Judaism does not really see God as sovereign but believes more in free will. They believe humans are blinded by sin and can't be instructed in righteousness. They believe salvation comes by following all the laws in the Torah. They believe in the bodily resurrection one day and in an earthly paradise but not necessarily that there is a hell.

CHRISTIANITY

Believe in one God, but in 3 persons of the Trinity. His nature is seen through His Son, Jesus. They believe we are dead in our sins and can only be rescued by the Holy Spirit, through belief in Christ. Christ purchased our sins and saved us through His sacrifice. If we believe in Him and follow Him and His teachings, God's grace is given to us and we are saved to be in heaven with Him immediately upon death, and then forever after bodily resurrection when Christ returns to earth again. Someday God creates a new heaven and earth where we live with Him. If you do not believe in Jesus and forgiven for your sins, you will live in eternal separation from God.

To summarize and explain; all religions cannot be true/all roads cannot lead to heaven because all religions are contradictory. They teach opposites. If one is true and the others teach opposites, then they must be false. If you compare the most important core beliefs of each religion, you can see that they either believe Jesus is God, or they do not believe He was God. So, if we can show everyone how Christianity is true, then all other religions must be false logically because they teach the opposite. Christianity among all religions has unique evidence from science, philosophy and history to show that God exists, the Bible is reliable, and Jesus died and was resurrected to save us. With those truths in mind, other religions are clearly false because they refuse to believe that. But this does not place Christians in arrogance but rather places a responsibility upon us to help others and to explain how Christianity is true and to help lead others to Christ.

ADJUST YOUR ATTITUDE

Scripture verses	Matthew 20:1-16
High level key topic	We have much to be grateful for

SCRIPTURAL LESSON NARRATIVE

This month's theme is about gratitude. Gratitude is when you let others know you see how they have helped you. Gratitude is important because we often tend to think that everything we accomplish is because of what we have done. In all circumstances, good or bad, we should pause and give thanks to God and to others for everything they do for us.

Even during bad times, remember that you still have Jesus, and give thanks. This simple act will also bring you peace and shows you trust God to help you through your difficulty. So pause and pray, and thank God for at least the opportunity to show you still trust Him. Ask Him to help you get through the difficulty. Then you will find a sense of peace by turning over your problem to God instead of stressing about it yourself. And when others do things for you, even the simplest things – thank them. Don't forget. This simple act of thanking others shows you know you can't make it through life strictly on your own. Everyone needs help from others and from God.

Today's lesson is about having a good attitude. There will be times when something happens and you think it is unfair. Maybe someone else receives something that you feel you should have had. Instead of complaining, or comparing yourself to others, adjust your attitude and focus on what you have. There will be many things in life that seem unfair. If you let yourself get caught up about those things, you will forget about all the good things and blessing you have that may not be fair when compared to someone else who is poor or handicapped. Adjust your attitude and recognize that God can do whatever He wants and allow whatever He wants to happen. But be thankful that you have God. Regardless of your circumstances or situation, adjust your attitude and be thankful that you have Jesus. Show God you trust Him by giving thanks even when things are bad or going wrong. Anyone can give thanks when everything is going right. It takes a mature, grateful Christian to give thanks to God when life is a struggle. There will always be struggles. So if you want to learn how to deal with them when they happen, start by giving thanks to God that you at least have Jesus. God is at work in our lives for our good, even when we don't see it. He is helping us learn, and grow, and build our character through trials. Always remember too that there is always someone else who has it worse than you. Remember your blessings.

In today's story about the workers and the landowner, most people's first reaction is that it isn't fair that some workers worked all day and were paid the same as a few who came late and only worked an hour. This lesson is all about realizing that you have a great blessing and should not compare yourself to others or feel that you should have more than others because you do more. This lesson is about God's grace. He gives things to those He chooses, and how He chooses. Instead of complaining that you deserve more or someone else deserves less, give thanks for what you have. Are the workers who worked all day still better off than if they had not worked at all? Don't be jealous of others who may have it easier than you or perhaps seemingly have more good things happen to them. You cannot know what other things may be going on in their lives that are much worse than your circumstances. Focus on what God gave you and be thankful.

REVIEW OF EVIDENCE AND CHALLENGES
TO GOD'S EXISTENCE

GOD EXISTS - EVIDENCE	CHALLENGES AGAINST GOD'S EXISTENCE
Creation of the universe	**Big Bang explains creation of universe**
• The universe had a beginning. Whatever caused the universe was outside of time, all powerful, all knowing, and immaterial – God	• No. Big Bang describes how it started. What caused the Big Bang? – whatever it was, it was timeless, all powerful and all knowing - God
Fine tuning of the universe	**Random chance explains fine tuning**
• Everything in the universe is perfectly designed to support human life on earth. Something all intelligent designed it to be that way - God	• No. Scientists agree that the fine tuning is so amazing it is beyond the possibility of chance. It has the appearance of design. What could be all intelligent to design such perfection? - God
Creation of first life	**Evolution explains how life was created**
• All living organisms have unbelievable complexity and within each cell the DNA contains enough information to fill 1000 sets of encyclopedias. But information is only known to come from an intelligent source - God	• No. Even if evolution was true, and macro evolution is not, it only describes what happens after first life began. It has no explanation for how first life began. It wasn't random chance and first life is so complex it is beyond chance. Information only comes from an intelligent source. What source could be so intelligent? - God
Existence of morals	**Morals are taught by society and our parents**
• Babies know right from wrong as early as 6 months. How could they? Because God wrote on our hearts the ability to know right from wrong	• But all parents teach different in all nations and societies. Yet somehow we all agree some things are absolutely wrong. If evolution is correct and we are just higher forms of animals fighting for survival of the fittest, why would we feel any obligation to do anything but for ourselves? – God has provided wisdom in our hearts to know basics of right and wrong for all people and cultures.
	Also – Miracles are not possible
	• But they are. Creation of the universe and first life clearly happened outside of natural law and by definition are miracles. And Craig Keener's book, "Miracles", documents thousands of modern miracles. If God exists, miracles are possible. Since we know they have occurred, God is the likely source of the miracles that happened.
	And – the problem of evil and suffering disproves God
	• No, a better question is why is there any good in the world because if evolution is true that we all fight selfishly for our own survival. There should be no such thing as compassion. But there is compassion.
	• Free will, sin and Satan are the main reasons for evil and suffering. People make bad choices that cause harm. But God makes good things happen from bad.

So now we conclude our first argument for showing that Christianity is true – God exists!

DECEMBER LESSONS

As mentioned, due to the infrequency of formal Sunday school classes in our church and in most churches, the content is less voluminous for December. Use any of the extra lessons at the back of this curriculum where needed to supplement lessons.

THE CHRISTMAS STORY	
Scripture verses	Luke 1:26-35, 2:1-20
High level key topic	The Messiah was foretold

SCRIPTURAL LESSON NARRATIVE

We're going to take some time to read about the birth of Christ today. Remarkably, it was predicted/prophesied over 700 years before that by Isaiah and Micah. In fact no prophecy that God ever gave a prophet in a message has ever been false. All have come true but some are still to be fulfilled.

There are 1817 prophecies in the Bible. Over 100 are about the Messiah and fulfilled by Jesus. Let's look at some of them:

1. Born of a woman – Gen 3:15, confirmed in Galatians 4:4

2. Born of a virgin – Isaiah 7:14, confirmed in Matthew 1:21

3. Would die 483 years after temple reconstruction – Daniel 9:24, confirmed to the exact year

4. Descendant of Abraham – Gen 12:1-3, confirmed in Matthew 1:1 and Galatians 3:16

5. From the tribe of Judah – Gen 49:10 confirmed Luke 3:23, 33 and Hebrews 7:14

6. Descendant of King David – 2 Samuel 7:12, confirmed Matthew 1:1

7. Born in Bethlehem – Micah 5:2, confirmed Matthew 2:1 and Luke 2: 4-7

8. Anointed by the Holy Spirit – Isaiah 11:2, confirmed Matthew 3:16-17

9. Announced by a messenger in advance – Isaiah 40:3, confirmed Matthew 3:1-2

10. Worked miracles – Isaiah 35:5-6, confirmed Matthew 9:35

11. Cleansed the temple – Malachi 3:1, confirmed Matthew 21:12

12. Rejected by the Jews – Psalm 118:22, confirmed 1 Peter 2:7

13. Die a humiliating death – Psalm 22 and Isaiah 53, confirmed Matthew 27:31

    a. Enduring rejection, mocking, piercing of hands and feet, crucifixion with thieves, praying for His persecutors, pierced in His side, burial in a rich man's tomb, casting of lots for his clothes, confirmed John 1:10-11: 7:5, 48, Matthew 27:12-19, 31, Luke 23:33, Mark 15:27-28, Luke 23:34, John 19:34, Matthew 27:57-60, John 19:23-24, Acts 2:31, Mark 16:6, Acts 1:9, Hebrews 1:3

14. Raised from the dead – Psalm 2:7 and 16:10, confirmed Acts 2:31 and Mark 16:6

15. Ascended into heaven – Psalm 68:18, confirmed Acts 1:9

16. Sitting at right hand of God – Psalm 110:1, confirmed Hebrews 1:3

Now let's read the Christmas story that began the fulfillment of these prophecies. Read Luke 1:26-35, 2:1-20.

PROPHECY

Prophecy is a prediction about the future. It is not guessing who wins the Super Bowl or if there will be an eclipse next month. It is a message from God communicated through his prophets who were messengers. It is a miracle.

Prophecy is not a proof of God's existence but it is an evidence for the truth and reliability of the bible. There are no natural explanations for these phenomena. But nonbelievers try to get around it by claiming the prophecies were written after the events occurred. That is partly why so many of them wish to dispute the historical record of when various books were written. Otherwise they are left with the explanation that the prophecies actually happened.

Amazingly enough Professor Peter W. Stoner who authored "Science Speaks" stated that the probability of just eight particular prophecies being fulfilled in one person is 1 in 10(17),i.e. 1 in 100,000,000,000,000,000). This statement was validated by the American Scientific Affiliation.

Professor Stoner went on to consider 48 prophecies and says the probability of Jesus Christ fulfilling 48 prophecies is the same as one person being able to pick out a colored grain of sand from any beach in the world – 6 times. Yet Jesus fulfilled over 100 individual prophecies that concern the Messiah. We don't need blind faith to believe in Christianity.

What this means to all of us is that because we have great evidence these prophecies were made and fulfilled, we must be prepared for the prophecies that remain to come true. That means that Jesus will return again one day to wipe out evil. We have no idea when that may occur so be sure of your salvation in Christ, and spread the gospel to others that they may have the same opportunity.

DAVID AND JONATHAN	
Scripture verses	1 Samuel 18:1-9; 19:1-7; 20:1-42
High level key topic	Honor others by putting them first

SCRIPTURAL LESSON NARRATIVE

This month we focus on honor. Honor is letting someone know you see how valuable they really are. God asks us not to look at people from the outside but rather the inside. God judges value by a person's heart.

Today's lesson is about putting other people's feelings and concerns ahead of your own. We hear a lot of talk these days about equality but God actually wants us to put other's needs ahead of our own, not equal.

Last week David was anointed to be the new King by the prophet Samuel. But it was not an immediate action. Saul was still king. After David volunteered and killed Goliath, he became an immediate hero to the people and Saul appointed him in charge of the army and brought him to the palace to live. God blessed him in battle and David led many great victories. When David and Saul would travel into a city after victory, everyone would should and praise Saul but praise David even more. That made Saul very jealous and he became very suspicious of David after that. Saul had a son Jonathan, who was a Prince and would be in line to be the next king after Saul but Jonathan was close friends with David and cared about him so much he actually gave him his robe and belt and sword and bow.

Saul decided to have David killed, but Jonathan scolded his father saying David had done nothing wrong and it would be a sin. Saul agreed and swore he would not hurt David. But an evil spirit came over him. First he put him in charge of more soldiers hoping he would die in battle, and then he promised his daughter in marriage to David but changed his mind. But a second daughter loved David and he allowed her to be married to him. One day in the palace Saul threw his spear at David and missed, then had his men chase him. But David escaped. Jonathan protects David and decides to talk with his father at a feast coming up. He tells David he will give him a sign once he knows what is going on. When David does not show up at the feast, which was a trick to get David to come so Saul could kill him, Saul becomes furious and sends his men to find David and kill him. He even throws his spears at Jonathan. But Jonathan warns David and helps him get away.

So the message for us is that Jonathan cared for his friend David and put his needs ahead of his own. Jonathan could have gone along with his father's plan to kill David so he could become a king in waiting even faster. But David was his friend and he refused to betray him. When you encounter situations in your life where you could be selfish and think of yourself first, what will you do? Suppose your best friend needs help to study for a test and he/she is not doing well in the class. Would you help them or only focus on your own needs to try to beat them in the grade and elevate yourself over them? What do you do when your brother or sister wants to watch a different TV program than you, do you let them and show your generosity or do you take control because you are older and do what you want instead? What is the better example to help you and they learn the value of honoring another person than by showing them they are valuable?

EVIDENCE FOR THE RESURRECTION

In our discussion of the evidence to show Christianity is true, we covered the evidence to show God exists and that the Bible is reliable and we can trust it.

We can know God exists because the scientific evidence points to God as creator of the universe, all life, and sustainer of all things. This is no vague claim but backed up by all the best evidence from science itself.

We know the Bible can be trusted because we have 5700 partial or full copies from the early centuries that compare to 95% accuracy. Any errors are accounted for from copying errors mainly. We also know the NT was written within 30-40 years of Jesus' resurrection because there is no mention of the temple destruction in AD 70. As the most important part of their lives for over 2000 years, certainly this would have been written about but since it was not it can only mean that the writings occurred before the destruction happened. We can know that what was written must be true because no writers trying to persuade others about the events they witnessed would write embarrassing and humiliating details about themselves and Jesus.

Then we showed the evidence that Jesus is God; not just a teacher and prophet as other religions say. He made several claims that He was the Christ or Messiah and did many things that only God had the authority to do such as forgiveness of sins and taking worship in His name.

Now we advance to the most important piece of evidence of all. Was Jesus resurrected from the dead? If He was, then He is our Savior and we are eternally saved when we accept Him as our Lord. If He was not, Christianity is meaningless and we are still dead in our sins without a Savior. So it is critical to Christianity. In fact, if there is sufficient evidence to show Jesus is resurrected, that evidence alone makes the case to show Christianity is true.

Rather than get into the controversial evidence, let's look at what we call the minimal facts. The "minimal facts" approach relies on presentation only of evidence that is strong; and second, that virtually all scholars on the subject, even skeptic scholars, grant each of the pieces of data. Some people who admit the

NT is historically reliable still object to the resurrection because they refuse to believe miracles are possible. We will cover that evidence in another lesson.

This evidence logically points to the resurrection as the best explanation to explain the facts. It is an argument called minimal facts and is based on the fact that virtually all Bible scholars agree with these facts.

1. Jesus died by crucifixion

The crucifixion is reported in all four gospels by four different authors, and by 5 non-Christian sources: Josephus, a well-known Jewish historian of the time; Tacitus, a Roman senator and historian; Lucian, a Greek satirist; Mara Bar-Serapion, a Stoic philosopher from Syria; and the Talmud, a Rabbinic Jewish text. In fact, John Domonic Crossan, the very critical scholar from the Jewish Seminar (not exactly an evangelical) said "That he was crucified is as sure as anything historical can ever be."

2. Jesus' disciples believed He rose and appeared to them

The disciples claimed it themselves and then transformed into aggressive preachers of the gospel to the point of martyrdom for all of them save John, who likely died on the Isle of Patmos. The Apostle Paul claimed it as well via the oral tradition recorded in the early creed, expressed in 1 Corinthians 15:3-8. The amazing change in the disciples' behavior is phenomenal in its own right as they had previously proven to be timid, even cowards when they scattered upon Jesus' arrest and disappeared during the crucifixion and denied knowing him. Once they believed they saw him, everything changed and they were courageous, dauntless and aggressive in spite of imprisonment, beatings, torture and execution. No one would put themselves through that for a lie unless they fully believed it. Seven ancient sources confirm that the apostles claimed they saw the Resurrected Jesus and were willing to suffer and die for their claims.

3. The Apostle Paul's transformation

He transformed from a major persecutor of the church into the Apostle Paul, one of the greatest messengers of the gospel of all time. What could possibly account for this? It was his encounter with the Resurrected Jesus, about two years later while travelling on the road to Damascus where he had orders to pick up Christians and take them back to Jerusalem for imprisonment. His subsequent preaching, suffering and martyrdom are attested in his church letters and by Luke, his assistant; Clement of Rome; Polycarp; Tertullian; Dionysius of Corinth and Origen, all well-known figures of the time.

4. James, brother of Jesus, also transformed

James was one of Jesus' brothers and sisters, reported in the gospels and by Jewish historian Josephus. James was not a believer or follower of Jesus, as documented in the gospels, prior to Jesus' resurrection. Along with Jesus' mother Mary, the Bible indicates (Mark 3:21, 31; 6:3-4; John 7:5) they thought Jesus to be mad and feared for his life at times. James is mentioned in the early creed of 1 Corinthians 15: 3-8 which states he was among those who saw the resurrected Jesus. After his witness of the Resurrected Jesus, he became a leader of the Jerusalem church (Acts 15:12-21; Galatians 1:19). Eventually James also died of martyrdom, attested by Josephus, Hegesippus and Clement of Alexandria.

Additionally: Three-quarters of scholars do accept the empty tomb as evidence. The resurrection is the most logical explanation for the empty tomb. The very fact that Romans claimed Jesus' body was stolen is evidence that the tomb was empty. In fact, scripture documents the Jewish leaders were concerned the disciples might steal the body and requested guard support at the tomb and were granted the request.

Other fine points. It was unlikely that a Jewish Sanhedrin member (Jewish religious council) would be invented and named as the person who requested Jesus' body, then arrange the burial tomb. Clearly he was well-known in the community and this story could easily be checked out for falsification. Nothing like that happened.

Women were the first to discover the empty tomb. Since women's testimony was not allowed in a court of law, it is quite unlikely this story was invented.

Finally, no natural alternative explanation for the minimal facts is more reasonable than those I shared. Some say mass hallucinations explain it or wild animals ate the body, or Jesus didn't really die and was somehow healed, or Barrabas was killed, not Jesus. But there is no evidence for any of these.

Remember also the overall purpose of Jesus' life was to be a sacrifice for us because of the fall and because we cannot save ourselves from sin.

The evidence is too compelling not to believe. Even the most critical bible scholar of the NT agrees with all the evidence but refuses to believe it actually happened because he doesn't believe miracles are possible. He says that animals ate the body instead. But there is no historical fact or story that discusses that. He bases it on the general fact that unclaimed crucified bodies were buried in shallow graves and sometimes animals were known to dig them up. But Jesus' body was not unclaimed. It is historically written that Joseph of Arimathea claimed it and put it in a tomb he owned. Everyone would have known where that was.

If the resurrection happened, it means Christianity is true. And that means it is critical for all people to take a knee and accept Christ as Savior. Amen.

HOPE

Scripture verses	Matthew 14: 22-33
High level key topic	Jesus is our hope for salvation

SCRIPTURAL LESSON NARRATIVE

The dictionary defines hope as the belief that what we want can happen or that whatever happens will turn out for the best. If you accept Christ as your Savior that is exactly the way it works. Several places in the Bible it tells us that whatever we ask for in Christ it will be given to us. That doesn't mean selfish and material desires or that your prayer will be answered exactly the way you request it. But it does mean that God is listening and will do the best thing for you based on your prayer as long as it fits within His plan for your life.

Hope is an invisible feeling that helps you keep on living when things look troublesome. What a powerful feeling it is to know that whatever happens the most powerful being in the universe is there to help you and will take whatever happens and make it good for your life. As long as we remember that we can have peace and not panic when our world seems difficult and things are not going our way. When your world is crumbling, focus on Jesus, give Him thanks, praise Him, and ask Him whatever you need. He will help you through and make things turn out better for you. You may not see it right away but it will happen.

When things are going badly we tend to panic and try to fix them. But we cannot control most of our circumstances. Instead of wasting energy and worrying about it, ask God to help us identify the most important thing to do next. Then rely on God to help you get through that day. When you learn to master living one day at a time in reliance on Jesus, you will learn the secret to having peace in your life.

In today's story, Jesus had just finished the feeding of the 5,000. Now He asked the disciples to cross the sea in their boat and meet Him on the other side while He went up the mountain to pray. When He finished, the boat was a mile out and a storm was upon them. Suddenly they saw Jesus walking across the water toward them and shouted to Him. Peter asked that Jesus command him to walk toward Him on the water. He did and Peter began to walk until He saw the power of the storm and became afraid then began to sink. He cried out "save me" to Jesus and Jesus took His hand, saying, "Oh ye of little faith. What were you afraid of?" The others in the boat were astonished and said, "Truly this man is the Son of God."

When we lose our focus on Christ, we begin to sink into life's problems and become afraid. Keep your eyes on Jesus and He will provide you the hope you seek to make it through your circumstances.

ARE MORMONS AND JEHOVAH'S WITNESSES CHRISTIANS, AND OTHER MODERN CULTS?

The dictionary defines cult as a system of religious beliefs and rites. But the general meaning of the word cult in religious terms is a deviation from the normal. And that is what Mormons, Jehovah's Witnesses, Christian Scientists and Scientologists, and others such as WICCA and New Age are. They do not represent traditional Christianity. They are abnormal variations from Christianity and are defined by the fact they do not believe in the Trinity and that Jesus is the Son of God.

Let's review them.

Mormons - also called LDS, or the Church of Latter Day Saints

Joseph Smith is claimed to be a modern prophet who established a new version of Biblical teaching. They have several books/scriptures of authority. They believe God the Father was a man elevated to rule the world and he himself had a father and mother and wife. He is the creator of all the spirits that will be born on earth. They believe in many gods. They believe that the fall of Adam and Eve was not a serious sin because it opened the way to perfection. They believe that we can overcome sin and please the Father. They believe Christ was conceived from a physical union between the Father and Mary. They believe he was married and had children and became a God when resurrected. They believe that Christ did not purchase our salvation. They believe our good works earn us most of the way to salvation, and then God's grace takes us the rest of the way. They believe in hell but it is not clear if anyone but Satan and his demons will spend eternity in hell. Some of them also believe if you reject Mormon teaching you will be in hell. They believe in three realms and only Mormons will be in the highest realm.

Jehovah's Witnesses - also called Watchtower Society

They have a variation of the Bible they created and believe you cannot understand the Bible without their help. They do not believe in the Trinity and think it is satanic. They don't believe the body and soul are separate and think that at death we go to sleep until the resurrection. They believe Jesus was the archangel Michael before becoming a man. They don't believe he was a God but only a perfect man then made immortal in the resurrection. They don't believe Christ's death bought our salvation but that we are saved by following their teachings. They believe those who do not repent of their sins die in the lake of fire but are not there eternally. They believe there are two other saved groups. One lives in heaven with God and the other on earth forever.

Christian Science – church of Christian Science

The Bible has authority but only as interpreted by their founder, Mary Baker Eddy. The trinity is a group of attributes not persons. God is an infinite mind. Humans are also just mind. Matter, sin, death and disease are not real. Christ is the spiritual element of God and came to show us how to be spiritual. They believe all are saved but that we should seek a level of enlightenment. They don't believe in heaven or hell but that we progress to greater levels of enlightenment. Mind and spirit are all that exist.

Scientology – Tom Cruise, John Travolta

Spiritual authority comes from the writings of L. Ron Hubbard. His source was eastern and Native American traditions. They believe God is what he is for each person. So he is different for each person. Hubbard's beliefs were a combination of Judaism, Christianity, and Hinduism. They believe man is partly god and composed of the physical and spiritual and is basically good. Each person has a Thetan spirit that is 80 trillion years old, that it survives death then implants itself into another person. Jesus has no role in this cult. We all go through reincarnation. When we develop enough spiritually we can understand our Thetan nature and cease the cycle of reincarnation and join the intergalactic Thetan collective.

You will observe that most of these teach some abnormal variation of the Bible and Christianity. That's the problem. The Bible itself tells us that antichrists will appear in the world with false teachings and that anything different than what the Bible says is not true. We must be on our guard against false teachings and false prophets who try to take us away from the real truth of Christ, God and the Bible. You will find difficult passages in the Bible to understand and difficult parts of Christianity. These mysteries will only be revealed when we are in heaven with God. Don't let yourself be deceived by false teachings. And for those teaching the false doctrine, either avoid them or try to help them understand the truth but do not let yourself get swayed from what you know to be the truth in Christ and God's Word.

THE GIFT IS BORN	
Scripture verses	Luke 2:1-20
High level key topic	Jesus is our hope for salvation

SCRIPTURAL LESSON NARRATIVE

We continue our studies about God's gift (Jesus) as He is born in this week's lesson. Try to keep in mind that Jesus was both God and man. His human form and attributes were added to His Godly attributes of omniscience, omnipresence, omnipotence, eternality, all holiness and all lovingness. When God stepped into our world in human form, it was because of how much he loved us and because He is a just and holy God and cannot tolerate sin. There was no other way to save us from our sins except through the sacrifice of Someone to pay the penalty for us. Understand that Jesus took all our sins on His shoulders to endure the punishment that should have been for us because of our sin. But when He did that the sins of all people past, present and future were wiped clean for all those who accept Him in their hearts as Lord and Savior, and who ask forgiveness and turn away from their sins.

In today's story, the Roman emperor Caesar Augustus called for a census in the region. In this case, it required everyone to return to their home towns to register. Joseph was a descendant of the house of David and therefore returned to Bethlehem, David's birthplace. Mary was pregnant with child and rode on a donkey on the long ride back there. Because of the census the town was overwhelmed with people and there was no room for Mary and Joseph to stay in regular lodging. Somehow they found someone who allowed them to stay in the stable where the animals were and when Jesus was born he was placed in a feeding trough.

Meanwhile, nearby shepherds were amazed, shocked, and scared when an angel appeared to them to announce that the Messiah had been born nearby. The shepherds went to see it all while a host of angels praised God. Remember that this baby Jesus grew to be a man, was God in human form, and that He specifically came to endure shame and torture, excruciating pain, and die just to save everyone from their sins. No price was needed to be paid by us as Jesus bore it all. Now we are cleansed of sin in God's eyes. We still sin and can't help ourselves but in God's eyes, once we accept Jesus, the slate is wiped clean. Because of this act of grace and unselfish love, how will you show God you love Him and thank Him? Keep Him in your heart and mind always. Share His gospel with others. Be obedient and follow His commands.

IS IT POSSIBLE JESUS WAS BORN OF A VIRGIN?

The idea that anyone could be born of a virgin has been challenged and criticized throughout history since the time of Jesus. A virgin birth means that there was no physical contact between the man and woman yet she became pregnant with child.

For nonbelievers and skeptics they say this is ridiculous and impossible and has never been proven to happen. So what evidence do we have that it happened?

1. Miracles are possible. Due to science's belief that every event has only a natural cause and because they believe there is nothing outside the natural world by definition they are not in position to comment on the supernatural. Of course they do anyway. But clearly miracles have happened because the creation of the universe from nothing was impossible yet it happened. And creation of first life has been proven to be virtually impossible from random chance and no other explanation even comes close other than God created the universe and life. So miracles are possible. The idea that the natural world is the only alternative is a logical fallacy. Logically, every cause is either natural or unnatural/supernatural. Yet they rule it out purely by assumption that is does not exist.

2. Prophecies. Gen 3:15, Jeremiah 22, Isaiah 7:14, verification of virgin birth in Matthew 1:18-23. Hundreds of years in advance it was predicted. Eyewitnesses testified. So it is no chance occurrence.

3. Historical reliability of the New Testament. It was recorded within a generation of Jesus by eyewitnesses or reporters who interviewed eyewitnesses. We have over 5700 Greek manuscripts surviving today that support the accuracy and integrity of scripture.

4. God exists and is all powerful. We have many lines of evidence that point to God's existence. Because of His unlimited power and eternality, He is easily capable of causing Mary to become pregnant. Compared to the creation of the universe and all life this is even a lesser miracle.

JANUARY LESSONS

Now that the fundamentals have been covered along with some popular related issues, from here on we will continue to mix in random related topics and also occasional reviews and repetition of major topics for emphasis. Remember, many children do not attend weekly so do not let yourself feel your teaching is repetitive. It is actually a good thing to repeat key lessons and ask more questions during those times to see if they remember.

APOLOGETICS REVIEW	
Scripture verses	1 Peter 3:15-16
High level key topic	Always be prepared to give an answer to those who ask you the reason for the hope you have. But do this with gentleness and respect. 1 Pet. 3:15

APOLOGETICS LESSON (DEFENDING CHRISTIANITY)

APOLOGETICS REVIEW
WHAT IS APOLOGETICS?
DEFENDING CHRISTIANITY BY SHOWING EVIDENCE THAT IT IS TRUE.

So far we discussed the following pieces of evidence to show that Christianity is true. What evidence do we have for each?

GOD

- The universe had a beginning and was created from nothing

- This is not scientifically possible from nature

- So whatever created the universe was beyond time, space and matter, and all-powerful

- This fits the Christian definition of attributes of God

Q. But what about the Big Bang, doesn't science show that is how the universe began?

A. No, the Big Bang did not cause the universe to exist, it describes it. What caused the Big Bang to happen? God

BIBLE

- The bible has proven to be reliable and what it teaches can be believed and trusted

- The NT was written within 20-30 years after Jesus death

- It was written by eyewitnesses to the events

- We have 5700 copies that agree to over 95% accuracy in what they say over several centuries

Q. But doesn't the Bible have hundreds of thousands of errors?

A. Yes but almost all are copying errors and grammatical errors. None affect any significant verses or meanings or doctrine.

Q. But we don't have an original of the Bible or any of the books so how can we know it is accurate?

A. When you compare all the manuscripts they tell the same story.

JESUS

- He fulfilled a hundred prophecies that no other person fits.

- He predicted his own death and resurrection and it happened.

- He claimed to be God directly and indirectly.

Q. But how do we know He was actually resurrected?

A. Over 500 eyewitnesses saw Him including all the apostles. Lives were transformed. The tomb was empty.

OTHER RELIGIONS

- Christianity claims that it is the only way to heaven. (John 14:6)

Q. But couldn't other religions be true?

A. No, not if Christianity is true. Because all other religions deny Jesus is God, then if Jesus is God, the other religions are false. That is why it is so important to know if Christianity is true.

CONCLUSION:

God exists, the Bible is reliable, Jesus is God and Christianity is true, so other religions cannot be true.

So we should share the gospel to help others accept Christ.

SELF-CONTROL	
Scripture verses	Proverbs 16:32 Whoever is slow to anger is better than the mighty, and he who rules his spirit than he who takes a city.
High level key topic	It's better to not get angry than do something you will regret

SCRIPTURAL LESSON NARRATIVE

Have you ever lost your temper? What happened? Did you feel better after you got mad and did whatever you did? What could you have done instead?

When we lose our temper it usually results in something bad happening. Someone gets hurt physically or emotionally and you will feel bad about it and maybe there will be consequences.

What is self-control? It is controlling you. It is choosing to do what you should do not what you want to do. Why do we lose our temper? Usually because we want something to happen our way or maybe we don't want something to happen that is about to. It comes down to wanting what we want and forgetting that others might be involved and maybe that God wants something different.

How do we keep from losing our temper? Well, first thing is to understand that losing your temper is bad and people will get hurt, including you. Then, understanding it is bad, we have to decide to do something about it. Third, we need to recognize when it is about to happen. Think back to that moment just before you lost your temper. Do you remember starting to have this building feeling of anger? That is when you need to stop yourself. When you feel yourself building up anger, stop and pause. Some people say count to ten. Whatever works. I recommend you say a short prayer and ask God to help you stay in control and not get upset and to know what to do next.

Have you ever been angry and wanted to get revenge or teach someone a lesson? How did that turn out? Did you feel better after or worse? Read James 1:19-21.

Often, listening instead of talking at that point can help. When you are listening you are in control. When you are talking your anger just keeps building and you are not thinking. Remember the golden rule: treat others like you want to be treated. So, if you wouldn't like it if someone said something hurtful to you or maybe hit you or pushed you, then you shouldn't do it either.

Let's talk about a few examples. What would you do in these scenarios?

- How can you handle your anger when you are frustrated at school because you forgot a homework assignment?

- How can you handle your anger when some kid at school is teasing and bothering you?

- How can you handle your anger at home when something happens and your parents misunderstand that it was not your fault but punish you instead?

- How can you handle your anger when your teammate messes up and you lose the game or match?

Maybe instead you can pray to God – be with me now God and help me keep from getting angry and know what to do. Help me to slow down, listen to you, and not lose my temper. Because that is what you want and that is what I want.

ISLAM

The issues about Islam and terrorists are in the news more and more. It will only get worse before it has a chance to get better.

Here are two key questions:

Do Muslims and Christians worship the same God?

The Pope has implied we do. Oprah Winfrey said so. President Obama thought so. Some Christian religious professors have said so. Even some Christian pastors have said so. But no, we do not worship the same God. Here's why:

- The Christian God loves sinners but the Islam God hates sinners. But everyone is a sinner so the Islam God hates everyone. That means they cannot be the same God because of the law of opposites.

- The Christian God offers salvation by accepting Jesus but the Islam God requires doing more good deeds than bad deeds to enter heaven. But there is no way to know how to do that and we will fail. Does one simple good deed cancel out a terrible bad deed? No. Even if somehow you did more good deeds than bad, the Islam God might decide otherwise anyway. So this is not the same God as Christianity.

- The Christian God does not cause people to sin but the Islam God controls everything and may cause you to sin and do evil. So they are not the same God.

Are the Muslims who commit terror following Islam and what their God wants?

Recently, a Muslim in Philadelphia ran up to a policeman in his car and fired 13 shots at him, hitting him in the arm three times. The policeman fought back and the Muslim was caught. He confessed he did it in the name of Allah and Islam and that his religion tells him that is the right thing to do. The police chief states all this on TV in a press conference. Then immediately after the mayor jumped in and said that incident had nothing to do with Islam and that nobody there believes it was about Islam. This is like a murderer saying he did it and the police detective saying no you didn't even though there is a video showing it happened. This is dangerous

- Our government and politicians say no the terror has nothing to do with Islam. The politicians don't want to hurt all Muslims' feelings by saying that those who kill in the name of Islam are bad. Instead, they say it has nothing to do with Islam. Just the other day in Philadelphia this happened. And many other times.

- But the politicians are wrong. They are not theology scholars. And the terrorists actually say they are doing it in the name of Islam. Yet the politicians want to say no they are not. The Muslim terrorists have over 100 verses in their holy scripture that tell them to kill non-believers and commit acts of violence. And they are doing exactly what the founder of Islam, Muhammed, did to get the religion started. So our politicians are just blind to what is going on.

- Conclusion: we cannot win a battle if we do not know what causes the enemy to hate us and kill us. It is their religion and nothing else. We will not overcome it only by killing them back. We have to get other Muslims to fight the battle with those who are hurting their religion and saying and doing wrong things. But until we openly admit that is the problem nothing will happen to change it.

GOD LOVES YOU	
Scripture verses	Matthew 9:18-31
High level key topic	God showed His love for us by sending Jesus to save us from our sins

SCRIPTURAL LESSON NARRATIVE

How do we know God loves us? Because God took the form of a human, endured unbearable punishment, torture and pain and death, just to take away our sins so we could live with God someday in heaven forever. Think about it. At any time while being tortured or on the cross in incredible pain, Jesus could have said one word and made it all go away but didn't. For if He had, Father God's plan for our salvation could not be fulfilled. So Jesus endured it for us.

The idea that a person could do that for us is hard to believe. But for an all-powerful being to do so is incomprehensible. But it happened. Now because it happened and because we are all God's children we must find it in our hearts to love others the way Jesus loves us. Sometimes that is difficult because we may meet someone we just don't like. Or someone may be mean to us and hurt us but we are still called to love them as a Christian brother or sister. We don't have to like them, just respect them and show them brotherly love and care about them and pray for them and even help them wherever we can.

Today's lesson is about several of Jesus' healing miracles. He healed partly to show his love and compassion for people and partly to show His power came from God so that people would believe. As He was travelling, a leader approached him and said his daughter was dying and that Jesus could save her. While on His way there, a woman approached Jesus and touched the tassel on His robe. She had a severe bleeding problem but when she touched the robe Jesus noticed and turned to her and said that she was healed because of her faith. Then Jesus reached the leader's house and the girl had already died. Jesus said no she was not dead but just sleeping. They laughed at Him. He went into her room, took her hand, and had her get up and she was alive. The news spread fast around the area. Later Jesus was travelling again and healed two blind men. He asked them not to say anything but they told everyone and the news spread. No one ever disputed these miracles although the Jewish leaders often accused the miracles performed to be evil coming from Satan.

Think about someone right now who you do not like and let's pray to God to ask us to soften our hearts and find it within us to pray for them and to feel compassion and Christian love for them and not harbor any hate or mean feelings for them.

WHY DOESN'T GOD ELIMINATE EVIL AND SUFFERING?

This is the most common objection that atheists and other nonbelievers have about God. Why would a loving God allow such pain and suffering and death in our world? If he is all powerful and all loving, why not wipe it out?

Well, the Bible promises us that indeed one day God will wipe out evil for good. But apparently, more things must happen in God's plan for that to occur. Perhaps we have much more to learn about becoming strong Christians before we are ready to be in heaven. Perhaps we have not yet reached the number of saved souls before the end of this world as we know it comes about.

Atheists often try to have it both ways. First, they say why does God allow evil? But then in some places in the Bible where God delivers judgment and wipes out evil in a particular area, like the Canaanites massacre or Sodom and Gomorrah, then they say God is not merciful and loving or He would not kill innocent men, women, and children and even allow genocide. But you can't have it both ways. These things are explainable. Let's examine.

First, the Canaanites spent 400 years worshiping other Gods and did not change their evil ways, even sacrificing babies and children to Molech, a satanic demon they worshiped as a god. So they were not innocent. But what about the children you say, certainly they were innocent. Some theologians say there is an age for a child where they are not yet held responsible for their understanding and belief in God, or lack thereof. So any under that age of understanding would go to heaven and be saved anyway. So technically, they are saved from worse fates and are safe and joyful in heaven.

But what about the Jewish soldiers God used to wipe out the Canaanites? How was that fair to use them to accomplish His plan and become mass murderers? Well, more needs to be examined. First, God never delivered an initial command to kill everyone. He told them to drive the Canaanites out. But when they stopped after a while and had not completed the mission, God then told them to remove all the remaining ones. It is perfectly within God's authority and sovereignty to do whatever He feels but He does not do things unjustly.

As for the rest of the discussion of the problem of evil and suffering, it has a lot to do with free will, and inherited sin. Because God gives us freedom of choice, sometimes we make bad decisions and choose to do evil. But there are good things that happen as a result of evil as well. In fact, the Bible tells us that God turns everything that happens into good for those who love Him.

What good can come from evil? Remember the story of Joseph, where his brothers planned evil but in the end Joseph said God planned the evil for good.

Beyond that how can one appreciate or even know what good is without seeing how bad evil is. It is only through comparison that we understand things. If there were no evil, pain and suffering, we would not understand that what was left was good and not appreciate it.

Think about the things we would not be able to understand or have, if there were no evil or bad things:

- We would not know what courage is if there was no fear

- Without suffering we could not experience and provide compassion

- Without pain we could not know what pleasure and joy are

Those are just a few examples. It is primarily through pain and suffering and trials that we grow and become stronger and better people and better Christians. Also, if there were no pain, evil or suffering, we would quickly become complacent and not even pay attention to God. We would not feel a need for God because nothing would be going wrong in our lives. It is because of problems that many people finally turn to God. In our weakness, God demonstrates His power and strength. So pain, evil and suffering are actually blessings because they make us turn to God and deepen our connection to Him and make us realize we cannot survive without Him.

DO YOUR PART

Scripture verses	Acts 11:19-30
High level key topic	Find ways to help serve God and others

SCRIPTURAL LESSON NARRATIVE

Ever wonder when the disciples were first called Christians? One of the disciples, Stephen, was stoned by the Jewish leaders for preaching the gospel. They thought the gospel was blasphemous (against God) because Jesus had claimed He was God and equal to God. After Stephen's horrible death, the early believers became scared and many left Jerusalem and scattered to other cities in all directions. They feared for their lives and the Jewish leaders and Roman soldiers continued to persecute them, hunt them down, imprison them, and execute them. We call this scattering phenomenon the diaspora. Ironically, although it sounds like Christianity was on the run, God used this scattering to spread Christianity even faster as they all settled in many different cities in the Middle East and began spreading the gospel there.

Antioch was the third largest city in the Roman Empire and many believers fled there. The gospel spread quickly and many believers were saved. This is the first time that believers became known as Christians (little Christs). Word of the growing group of believers got back to the disciples left in Jerusalem and they were excited. They sent Barnabas, one of the key disciples, to Antioch to help teach them. After a while, Barnabas went to find Paul and brought him back to Antioch and together they spent a year teaching and sharing with the new believers there. Then a prophet named Agabus emerged and predicted a great famine would occur in Jerusalem soon. The Antioch believers were moved and put together many supplies to send back to those in Jerusalem.

So that is our message. Give and be a part of serving God's purposes and helping others. How can you give your part to the church and others? Offering, your time, your prayers, spending time and sharing are a few ways. God doesn't need your money. He will accomplish His purposes with or without it. The giving is for our benefit and to show our appreciation for what God does. But the command is there for us to help others and follow God's commands so by giving you show your respect for God and His teachings and your recognition that you have a giving heart

GRACE vs GOOD WORKS

How are we saved, by God's grace or by doing good works? Let's take two different people and examine their lives. One is raised in the church, becomes a Christian, loves the Lord, helps others and tries to follow God's commands and to serve others. When he falters he prays for forgiveness. He lives a good life his whole life, recognizes his failings but always asks forgiveness. One day he dies in very old age.

The second person grows up without God, doesn't go to church, ignores God his whole life and even does some evil things. He is selfish, doesn't help others, doesn't believe God, and even ridicules those who are believers. He lives a long life with nothing gained spiritually. At a very old age, on his deathbed, realizing the error of his ways his whole life, a family member shares the gospel one more time with him, he recognizes how foolish he has been, prays for repentance and forgiveness and acknowledges Jesus as Lord and Savior. And he is saved.

Is that fair?

Whether we decide it is fair or not, this is the way God's grace is. Grace is a free gift that we cannot earn. We don't deserve it but God gives it to us anyway if we will only believe in Christ, repent of our sins, and follow him. When we do so we are saved and will be with Christ eternally. Nothing can prevent that and no one can earn it any other way. Certainly God would prefer you are like the first man so that you have a chance to do good things in your life because you recognize what Christ did for you. But God does not allow someone like the first man to boast to others about his good works and believe that he had earned his salvation.

There are many examples of grace and good works discussed in the Bible. Two parables come to mind: the story of the prodigal son and the story of the workers. The prodigal son is about a young man who took all his inheritance early and recklessly spent it all and lived a foolish life. When he realized his foolishness he returned to his father to beg forgiveness. His father welcomed him with a feast and that upset his brother who had faithfully remained with his father and did good the whole time. The father explained to the jealous son that he thought his other son was dead but was now alive so that brought joy. He explained that the jealous son always had whatever he wanted from the father but the reckless son had returned. This is the way God sees us also.

In the story of the workers, a master hired many workers for the fields early in the morning and promised them all a day's wages. Late in the afternoon another worker showed up and the master put him to work and even gave him the same daily wage as the others. Does that seem fair? This is how God views the examples of the good and evil man I explained earlier. In God's eyes, we are all equally loved and whether we accept Christ early, middle, or late in our lives He loves us equally.

But be careful if you think that you can recklessly live your lives then be saved at the end. It doesn't work like that. God knows your heart and does not allow it to happen that way. Although we have free will, our salvation is complete only through the Holy Spirit. Only when the Holy Spirit recognizes that our heart is ready, then we are saved. If you consciously ignore God your whole life thinking you will accept Christ when you are ready, the Holy Spirit recognizes your insincerity and the timing may never happen for you to be moved to salvation. Our moment of acceptance and salvation is done in combination with the Holy Spirit, not on our own. So, don't ever wait if you feel ready to accept Christ, and if a friend or loved one says something similar, convince them not to wait because when the moment arrives it must happen at that time.

FEBRUARY LESSONS

APOLOGETICS REVIEW	
Scripture verses	Genesis 1:1-2:4
High level key topic	God created the universe and all that is in it

SCRIPTURAL LESSON NARRATIVE

In today's lesson, we discuss the most amazing miracle of God – His creation of the universe. It is so significant we will review it and compare it to the science record to show that, contrary to many opinions, the Bible does not contradict the scientific record for how things were created. In fact, nature is God's expression of truth in the universe and the Bible is God's expression of truth through His word. He would not allow those to contradict. So, whenever we have an apparent contradiction, either we have not correctly interpreted the language of scripture properly or science is wrong or a bit of both. Be sure of it. Finally, we will tackle the still controversial topic of the age of the earth. Is it 6,000 years old as some Christians say (Young Earth/YE), or is it billions of years old as most scientists and other Christians say (Old Earth/OE). You should study the evidence yourself and decide.

Let's start by tackling what caused the universe to begin. This is still a mystery to science. Many brilliant scientists have written about this and tried to explain away the problem that the universe had a beginning therefore it requires a cause. This is the scientific law of causality. Every effect has a cause. Scientists have known since the early 90's with great certainty now that the universe had a beginning. But they have struck out trying to explain how something was created from nothing. Science has shown that when the universe began, all time, matter and space were created. They did not exist prior to that. They were created out of nothing. We know scientifically that is impossible. This is actually a great proof for God. Whatever caused the universe to begin existed before time and matter and space existed. So it is timeless, eternal and all-powerful to have created something out of nothing and to exist outside of time. It is easy to see this corresponds with the Christian concept of God. Many scientists are atheists so they do not like this conclusion and continue to fight against it by developing wild theories with no evidence.

Next, many scientists say the Bible's account of Genesis is completely wrong compared to the scientific evidence. However, they have not correctly understood what they read in the Bible. Upon further review, Genesis corresponds perfectly and in perfect chronological order to how the creation events occurred. This is miraculous in itself because Moses, the presumed author of Genesis, lived thousands of years ago and he knew almost nothing about science. Clearly God gave him enough knowledge to record a basic description of the creation events. Let's examine them.

Creation begins with Gen 1:1: "In the beginning, God created the heavens and earth." That says it all. The Bible predicted thousands of years ago that our known world had a beginning. No other religious scripture makes such a claim. If you think through logically how our world would need to be prepared and created in order to accommodate life, including human life, it is truly remarkable how it all occurred and that the Bible got it right. The Hebrew verb for created is 'bara' and always appears in the Bible associated with only one subject – God. It means something was brought into existence that did not exist before.

Day 1. Then Genesis 1:2 gives us a critical hint that many scientists fail to understand. The spirit of God was hovering over the waters. So the perspective is already from our earth, hovering above the water. This is important because next God says "let there be light". Scientists object to this saying it is out of order and that light was created the moment the universe began. Two issues here: first, the Hebrew word used here is not 'bara' but rather 'haya', which means exist or come to pass. It does not mean initial creation of light. As the Holy Spirit is hovering above the waters, it is easy to see that God began this process by clearing away the opaque earth's atmosphere and changed it to translucent and some light was now allowed to come in and shine on the earth. The light was already there but the initial earth was dark and hidden by clouds. God created physical light at the moment the universe began and this corresponds with science. From there the earth's atmosphere made some further remarkable scientific changes that could not be accounted for and it appears now that an asteroid collision with a young earth sent huge masses of dust into orbit and eventually consolidated into our moon after gravity went to work. It explains how the atmosphere became transparent as it is now. Now as sunlight somewhat comes through, day and night are distinguished from each other and we are able to begin tracking time and events.

Day 2. As the atmosphere changed, evaporation and water condensation began, creating a minimal water cycle and allowed for photosynthesis to begin. The atmosphere separated into a troposphere, stratosphere, mesosphere and ionosphere. Psalm 148 even distinguishes between the highest heavens and the water above the skies and says God put them in place.

Day 3. Initially the whole earth had been covered in water but now through tectonics the ocean floors rose and land began to appear. In fact we know at one time there was one great land mass and that eventually it drifted apart due to volcanic activity and plate tectonics into the continents we now have. Genesis refers to the gathering of the surface water to one place. More remarkable is that the land and water became a ratio perfect to form the maximum diversity and complexity of life; 29% land and 71% water. Science confirms this is ideal. Now with photosynthesis in place and water and land prepared, God brings forth vegetation. The Hebrew word 'dasha' means produce and could mean that God allowed the seeds to take a natural course to become plants. But from there, plants have not shown a natural way of producing other plant species on their own so God may have intervened to make that happen with the diversity of plants we have now.

Day 4. Although the earlier described atmospheric changes allowed light to begin shining through, it would be more like an overcast cloudy day. Now with vegetation begun, more light is needed and God allows the light of the sun and moon to show through, making sunny days possible and propelling vegetative life. In addition, the rotation rate of the earth slows to allow tolerant weather patterns. Another amazing coincidence occurs here as plants pull enough carbon dioxide out of the atmosphere to avoid the disaster that may have occurred on Mars. By pulling carbon dioxide from the atmosphere, plants prevented a deadly mixture of carbon dioxide and atmospheric water from forming into carbonic acid, which would have killed everything and caused the earth to become frozen as Mars is. Instead, volcanic and tectonic activity drove these carbonates deep beneath the earth's surface. But since then tectonic activity has dropped by 80% of what it was then, so that delicate life was made possible to be supported. Then God allowed the sun and moon to shine through, and other stars. They were already there but their light was not visible. The Hebrew verb 'asa', meaning completed action is used, not 'bara', meaning original creation.

Day 5. With all this in place, God moved next to create lower vertebrates such as fish and other ocean creatures, small animals and birds. On this day God is clearly preparing the final touches before He brings Adam and Eve onto the scene. Then finally on day 5 God created "soulish" animals, such as birds and other type animals that possess attributes of mind, will and emotions to some degree. Here the words 'bara' and 'asa' appear, suggesting God created some spontaneously and others perhaps were made from existing resources.

Day 6. Now God begins making land mammals. The Hebrew verb 'asa' is used which means made to happen, not originally created. These mammals include livestock and creatures that move along the ground, and wild animals. Although the Bible does not mention dinosaurs, these were probably created during day 6 as they went extinct some 65 million years ago, before humans arrived on the scene. To be clear, dinosaurs never existed at a time when humans did, contrary to some popular movies and stories about cavemen and dinosaurs. Finally, God creates Adam and Even in the image of God, and tasks them with ruling over the earth and all that He created. Image means similar attributes such as intelligence and emotions and reasoning, not necessarily physical appearance. God commands them to be fruitful and multiply.

Day 7. The Bible says that God rested on day 7. It does not mean He was tired or weary. The Hebrew word 'shabat' means ceased. So God ceased from His work of creation. In fact, scientifically we know that all the major animal groups were created about 543 million years ago during a five million year period called the Cambrian explosion from that period of time called Cambrian period. God finished his creation and no new animals were created after that. Since that time, no new phyla (body plans) have ever been discovered that were created after that period of time. So in fact, science agrees with the Bible that God rested from His work of creation. Amazing! The Bible confirms we are still in the seventh day and that it has not ended. Psalm 95:7-11, John 5:16-18, and Hebrews 4:1-11. Revelation 21 reveals the seventh day will come to an end.

YOUNG EARTH OR OLD EARTH?

Finally, let us have a brief discussion about the <u>controversy of the age of the earth</u>. Was the earth created in 7 literal 24 hour periods of time as some Christians say (YE), or billions of years as science says (OE)? Experts and church fathers have been split between their belief in a long day or a 24 hour view. The King James Version inaccurately replaced two Hebrew verbs for evening was and morning was for the evening and morning were the first day. This error led people to construe it as a 24 hour day. But the Hebrew words for evening and morning are 'ereb' and 'boquer' and some scholars would say they can also mean end of the evening and end of the day. Clearly since day 7 was not a 24 hour day there is little reason to believe the other days were 24 hour days. Additionally, when you read Gen 2:4, the entire creation period is described as a day, so that is not 24 hours.

The Hebrew word for day is 'yom' and carries multiple definitions for the time period and one is for a longer period of time. But it could be used to refer to the part of the day when it is light out or to a 24 hour day as well. You have to examine other places in the Bible where 'yom' is used to come to a conclusion. The fact is that it could be used either way and so the controversy about how long the day is becomes unnecessary. But many Christians still say and teach that the earth is 6000 years old, tracking the genealogy of descendants and concluding that is the amount of time, then disagreeing with scientists and forcing arguments unnecessarily. The Bible supports either view. Instead of alienating scientists and making Christians look foolish by claiming things that science has overwhelming evidence for, we should maintain a neutral position and focus on the key to Christianity – the Resurrection of Jesus. We can never engage someone in that conversation if they think we are so foolish to believe the earth is only 6000 years old. Christians should learn a lesson about this. In fact, this is the reason we cannot teach creationism in our schools. When the legal debates took place in court to settle this issue, the Christians who debated it were YE and made to look foolish by the scientists who refuted their stories and the judges agreed. Perhaps one day we will learn from this mistake and again have a chance to teach creationism along with evolution in our schools.

To conclude, the majority of all scientific evidence points toward the God of the Bible as the creator of the universe and all life. Because of that, we should pay attention to the rest of what the Bible says very closely, especially the information about Jesus. That is information that is the key to our salvation and cannot be obtained without accepting Him.

JESUS AMAZED HIS CRITICS

Scripture verses	John 9:1-34
High level key topic	Jesus did miracles to provide proof of who He was and to glorify God

SCRIPTURAL LESSON NARRATIVE

Jesus was walking by and found a blind man. His disciples asked, "Was it this man or his parents who sinned to cause his blindness?" In those days they believed if you were handicapped it was due to sin. Jesus said neither but that the man was put there to display the power of God today. Jesus spit on the ground and made it into mud and put it on the man's eyes and told him to go wash in the pool of Siloam. This was a test of faith since Jesus could have just made a command and made it happen. But the man did so and was healed and went around telling everyone about it. But they weren't sure it was the same man who had been blind. The Pharisees (Jewish religious council) found out and brought the man in. He told them the story but they didn't believe him.

They asked him who the man was and first he said it was Jesus. Then he said it was a prophet. Then he said it must be a man from God for who could do such things unless from God. But the Pharisees refused to believe and said it could not be a man of God for it went against the laws of doing things on the Sabbath. So they brought in his parents and asked them. They acknowledged the man had been blind at birth but did not know who did it. They threw the blind man out.

At the end of the story Jesus found the blind man again and explained who he was and the man said he believed. Jesus told the Pharisees that they could not believe because they were blind. The Pharisees were trying to say that they were not blind because they thought that would mean they were with sin. But by saying they were without sin they were really committing sin and were misguided about sin. This story is about having faith in God even though you may think you are in a desperate situation. This story is about those who see God's power and still refuse to believe. Although we may not recognize miracles today, we can still have faith and believe because of what we know God has done in the past and because of what He does in our lives and the world. Have faith and believe in Jesus.

TOP 3 CRITICISMS OF CHRISTIANITY

There are many others but here are the most common:

1. The problem of evil and suffering. Why would a loving God allow bad things to happen to good people? This is the most difficult and most common criticism. Instead we could say if there is no God why do good things happen? The simplest answer to the problem of evil and suffering is that God gave us free choice. Sometimes people make bad choices and do evil things. If God takes away our free choice, then we cannot freely choose Him and we are merely robots. Other explanations include the consequences of Adam and Eve's sin which caused everyone to have sin in their lives; also the possibility that this world was created to have the least amount of evil while still allowing us free choice; and the fact that we can only understand that something is evil if we measure it against the ultimate standard of goodness – God. So we can only see God's goodness and love because we can see the opposite effects -evil and bad.

2. Faith is irrational. Many say faith is belief in something that is unseen and that is foolish. They say there is no reason or evidence or proof behind the claims of Christianity. But faith is actually belief in something unseen because of what we can see. We can see the amazing world and life that God created. It is so complex it is beyond belief that it all happened through chance and nature. And in fact Christians do have good answers for the criticisms made against our belief in God. There is substantial philosophical, scientific and historical evidence to show God exists, the Bible is true, and Jesus was real, was God, was crucified and resurrected, so we can believe in Him.

3. Science provides all the answers so God is not needed to explain things. But this is not true. Science lacks many answers to some of the most important philosophical questions in life such as: How did the universe begin? How did first life begin? Where does the concept of beauty and love come from? How do we explain human consciousness? If there is nothing in the world but things produced from nature, then all we are is molecules in motion and our thoughts are merely random chemical reactions, then why should we believe anything we believe at all? In fact this shows that it is more irrational to believe that nature has all the answers.

Scripture verses	John 20:1-8
High level key topic	Does the shroud provide archaeological proof of Jesus' crucifixion?

APOLOGETICS LESSON (DEFENDING CHRISTIANITY)

SHROUD OF TURIN

Google for "shroud of turin" to show images to students.

Is it the actual burial cloth of Jesus? Does it prove Jesus existed and was crucified?

The image shows:

1. Pierced wrists and feet with real human blood (Mt 27:35, Lk 23:33, Mk 15:24-25, Jn 19:18,23)

2. A wound in his right side the size of a Roman *lance* associated with blood and a clear watery substance (Jn 19:34)

3. At least 30 wounds on his head matching wounds expected from a crown of thorns piercing the scalp (Mt 27:29, Mk 15:17, Jn 19:2,5)

4. Lack of broken legs unlike the corpse of Yehohanan (a Jewish crucifixion victim from the 1st century found in 1967) (Jn 19:31-33)

5. Swelling about the face from being beaten, in some cases by a hard long object like a rod (Mt 26:67, 27:30, Mk 14:65, Lk 22:63-64, Jn 18:22)

6. At least 120 scourge marks on his back and legs matching the impressions a Roman flagrum would leave (Mt 27:26, Mk 15:15, Jn 19:1)

7. Evidence a large heavy object was placed across his shoulders, after the scourging, matching historical accounts that Roman crucifixion victims were made to carry the cross beam of their cross (Mt 27:32,Mk 15:21, Lk 23:26, Jn 19:17)

8. Wrapped in a new clean linen cloth (Mt 27:59, Mk 15:46, Lk 23:53, Jn 19:40)

9. A man matching the traditional look of Jesus depicted in ancient art

Medical facts evident from the image:

1. Actual human blood of type AB is found on the Shroud. X and Y chromosomes were found showing the blood is male. The DNA is degraded like most ancient DNA.

2. The blood shows evidence of clotting with serum present too. The serum evidence is not visible to the eye, particularly on the scourge marks, and is not missing from any of them.

3. The blood is thicker than a healthy human and shows evidence of low oxygen content consistent with asphyxiation caused by crucifixion. The color and blood chemistry are consistent with crucifixion.

4. Blood flows on the scalp are anatomically correct showing both venous and arterial flows corresponding to the frontal vein and superficial temple artery.

5. The "watery" fluid around the side wound is from either the pericardial sac or pleural cavity (pleural effusion) consistent with what surgeons and doctors agree happens during crucifixion.

6. No decomposition stains are on the shroud, unlike other ancient burial cloths, which means the body left the shroud before decomposition occurred.

7. The thumbs are not visible which is consistent with research performed on cadavers showing that a nail driven through the wrist will cause the thumbs to draw up especially when hung under the weight of the body.

8. The rib cage is abnormally expanded and the pectoral muscles are drawn up toward the collar bone, consistent with crucifixion.

9. The abdomen is distended and the epigastric hollow is drawn in, again consistent with what would be expected of a crucifixion victim.

10. The femoral quadriceps and hip muscles are protruded consistent with crucifixion.

11. The body image is in rigor mortis evident from: the feet are in the crucifixion position rather than a resting position, the posture of the legs is bent, the thumbs are drawn in, the head is tilted slightly to one side and forward, the chest and abdomen are frozen in their crucifixion position

and there is no flattening of the buttocks and thighs from the weight of the body (they are in a stiff position).

12. Scrapes to the knees, nose and cheek were found, consistent with a possible fall from the weight of a heavy object on the shoulders. Dirt was also found in these areas.

13. The weight on the shoulders came after the scourging because the scourge marks are deformed in this area.

14. The scourge marks are outlined with serum from clotting blood which is invisible to the naked eye and there are more than a hundred of them. This seems inconceivable as an artist's detail.

15. The wound in the side is post-mortem evident from: there is no swelling like there is on the face and scourge wounds; the blood flow is smaller than it would have been alive, and the blood flow shows evidence of oozing.

16. Many of the blood flows are likely from oozing caused by moving a dead body. The directions of the blood flows also show multiple positions of the body including blood flows down both arms at angles of 55-65 degrees consistent with crucifixion.

17. The cloth is not damaged in the areas where there is dried blood like would be expected from removing a bandage stuck to a wound. The body left the cloth without disturbing the blood stains.

18. Multiple states of blood (venous, arterial, clotting, pre-mortem, post-mortem, low oxygen content from physical exertion) are beyond the knowledge of a medieval forger. A forger putting blood on the shroud would not have known there was any detectable difference to different states of blood and wouldn't even know where to put the different blood in the correct places on the shroud.

19. The image makes it possible to do a photo autopsy of Jesus to see if it matches actual damage done by crucifixion, which it does. Anatomical details of a dead body are too accurate for a forger in the 12th or 13th century.

20. The conclusion is that the shroud wrapped a real dead human body.

Other evidence the Shroud is authentic:

1. Of the 58 pollens found on the Shroud, only 17 are from France and It-

aly. 18 are from Edessa and 13 are from Constantinople. The rest are from Jerusalem. The pollens are only available at different times of the year and some are insect pollinated (rather than airborne). Considering these facts and the very limited displaying of the Mandylion and Shroud, pollen evidence is strong proof the Shroud has been in Jerusalem, Edessa, Constantinople, France and Italy, just the right places to correspond to the burial cloth of Jesus and the Mandylion. Since the history of the Shroud begins in France and it has never been anywhere but France and Italy since then, critics of its authenticity must explain why pollens from Turkey and Jerusalem are on it. Pollen evidence would never have entered a forger's mind.

2. Images of flowers appear on the Shroud that match flowers in Jerusalem. One species, Capparis aegyptia, blooms from Dec to Apr and the image matches the shape the flower would be after 24-36 hours of wilting and blooming about 3-4 in the afternoon.

3. An image of a coin over the right eye matches a coin minted by Pontius Pilate from 29-32 AD. The image even includes a minting error (known to exist) using the letters UCAI rather than UKAI. Jews were known to put coins over the eyes of the dead. King Agrippa coins from 41 AD were found in the skull of a woman in an ossuary in the tomb of Caiaphas, the high priest at the time of Jesus.

4. The image of the shroud matches Jewish burial practices that existed only in the 1st and 2nd century including: using one long burial cloth, putting flowers with the body, coins on the eyes, using a facial cloth to bind the chin, and being naked.

5. The plants identified by their images on the Shroud grow together in only one place, Jerusalem.

6. The weave of the cloth existed in the 1st century as an expensive weave.

7. The standard measure used in the 1st century was the Assyrian cubit. Using this measure the Shroud measures 8 x 2.

8. Limestone found on the Shroud matches the two locations where the possible tomb of Jesus is. That form of limestone is rare.

9. A face cloth known as the Sudarium (housed in Oviedo, Spain) has matching blood marks and pollen grains and has existed since at least 840 AD. That indicates the Shroud has existed since at least that time.

BE KIND TO FAMILY AND FRIENDS

Scripture verses	Ruth 1 and 2
High level key topic	Treat others the way you want to be treated

SCRIPTURAL LESSON NARRATIVE

The theme this month is kindness. Jesus showed kindness to everyone, even those who were poor, sick, enemies and those who sought to hurt Him. Because Jesus displayed kindness so frequently to everyone, we know that kindness is part of the character of God. Father God has been very kind to us by showing us how much He loves us, with all the blessings He gives, and in sending Jesus to be our Savior. Jesus showed His kindness to us by sacrificing Himself and taking the full punishment of our sins. So then should we show kindness to others because of all the kindness Father God and Jesus have shown to us?

In today's story, one kind act turns into more and more by others. A woman Naomi is married and has two sons. Her sons marry. But all the men die and the women are left widowed. This was very dangerous in those days because women had no rights and no way to make an income. The mother, Naomi, tries to convince her daughter-in-laws to return to their mothers and people because she will not be able to provide for them and because they are still young and need to find husbands again.

But one daughter-in-law, Ruth, refuses to leave Naomi and even swears an oath to stay with her to death. They travel to a part of the country where she knows people have food and she has some relatives there. Ruth goes into the fields to gather grain to make bread. She picks up the leftovers from the harvest as they fall on the ground. But the owner of one of the fields, Boaz, notices her and discovers how she refused to leave Naomi and Boaz realizes she is a relative of his and decides to help her. So he arranges for her to pick the grain in his field with his young women to keep her safe from any men who might harass her. And he invites her to eat with him in the evening. Ruth takes the leftover grain from the day and gives it to Naomi. Naomi realizes that Boaz has helped her and lets Ruth know that he is a good relative of theirs and will protect her.

What kindnesses have been shown?
- Ruth stayed with Naomi to help her
- Naomi took Ruth with her back to her homeland
- Ruth offered to work in the fields to get food for both of them
- Boaz provided care and support for Ruth

Let's pray. Lord, thank you for showing us what kindness is by sending Jesus as an example. Please help us to know how to show kindness to our family and friends. Amen.

MEET THE SKEPTIC

Let's stop for a moment in our lessons about the evidence that shows Christianity is true and review. Today, I will be the skeptic or non-believer and will make criticisms or raise issues that challenge Christianity and you will try to address my concerns.

1. Faith is belief in something that is unseen and with no reason or evidence. It is irrational and silly.

   a. Wrong. Faith is belief in what is unseen because of what we can see. Our faith is not blind but based on real evidence.

2. The natural world is all there is. Science can explain everything in the world today. There are no spirit beings or gods. These are all made up fantasies.

   a. Science cannot explain beauty, love and consciousness, so where do they come from? If not the natural world, then it must be the unnatural world.

3. The Big Bang disproves God.

   a. Wrong. It proves God. The Big Bang only describes how the universe was created. What caused the universe to come into existence? The most likely explanation is God because something was created out of nothing by an all intelligent, all powerful, timeless force. This is a close description of God.

4. Evolution is a fact.

   a. Micro evolution is probably a fact. Things change over time. Macro evolution has almost no evidence. It cannot explain all the different species.

5. Evolution explains where humans come from.

   a. The only way scientists can claim this is by classifying humans with other bipedal apes. But it is a misclassification since we have so many unique traits and there is no common ancestor found that links apes and humans.

6. Even if there was a God, perhaps all religions are true since they all worship a god.

   a. Wrong. Because religions contradict each other, they cannot all be true. If Christianity is true, then all other religions are false because they teach opposites. If Jesus is God, then other religions are false.

7. The Bible can't be trusted because it is made of myth and legends and stories with no proof.

   a. Wrong. We have thousands of copies that agree with only minor differences, and some copies that date to within the generation of Jesus. The New Testament is historical and most scholars agree.

8. Miracles are not possible

   a. Wrong. The creation of the universe and of first life are two of the greatest miracles that have happened. They both most likely occurred apart from nature so they are unnatural. And check out Craig Keener's book, "Miracles", that documents thousands of modern miracles from all over the world.

9. There is no evidence to show Jesus was even a historical figure.

   a. Wrong. Jesus is referred to many times from 11 non-Christian sources including Josephus, a famous Jewish historian of Jesus' time.

10. Jesus was not resurrected.

    a. But the evidence points persuasively to the truth of His resurrection.

       i. The tomb was empty

       ii. We know he died and was buried.

       iii. There were over 500 witnesses to His resurrected body through a dozen appearances over 40 days after His death, including eyewitnesses from all the apostles and later Paul.

If a skeptic is sincere in their disbelief because they do not believe there is evidence, then how will they respond when shown the evidence? Will they accept Jesus as Savior and have their lives transformed? If not, they should be skeptical of being a skeptic.

MARCH LESSONS

PATIENCE	
Scripture verses	Genesis 25:24-34
High level key topic	God is patient with us so we should be patient with others

SCRIPTURAL LESSON NARRATIVE

The theme this month is patience. Patience is when you wait for something that you want now. Have you ever been on a trip and asked your parents multiple times, "are we there yet?" God has shown patience with us. Remember that He could have wiped out Adam and Eve but he only disciplined them. Remember how the Israelites in the Old Testament kept turning their backs on Him. But He did not wipe them out. Only when everyone except Noah's family had turned evil did God take action. That was perhaps 1000 years God waited. He sent Jesus to save us from our sins because He knew we would not have the patience to keep ourselves from sin. Patience often affects our relationships with others. If we lose our temper and yell at a family member or friend, it can hurt their feelings and hurt your relationship.

The suggested solution to help you have more patience is: when you think you can't wait, think twice. There is an old saying, "Lord give me patience and I want it now." We live in a time where we want it all and want it right away. We don't like to wait for things to happen. How about your prayers? Do you get uncomfortable if you don't see an answer to a prayer right away, and just the way you want the answer to come?

Often times we pray about things over and over, but can you wait weeks, months, even years until your prayer is answered? Many people cannot. Remember that God's timing is always perfect. Yours is not. So when you pray for something, trust that God heard you and has already worked out an answer. Be patient and wait.

When you have a big decision to make about whether to do something or not, pray about it. But if you don't hear or feel that God gives you an answer to your decision, perhaps that is his answer: do nothing. The psalmist said, "Be still and know that I am God". Try to remember this when struggling about whether to make an important action or step to do something. But even if you do the wrong thing, God will help you through the consequence of your action. Sometimes that involves discipline and testing, and learning lessons. The most important thing is to call on God in prayer before you make any important decision. Then trust Him for whatever outcome happens.

Today's lesson is a classic example of someone who had no patience. You may know the story of Jacob and Esau. Esau was a hunter and Jacob liked to work around the house. Esau came in one day after hunting and was starving. He asked Jacob to make his favorite stew for him. Jacob saw an opportunity and asked him to swear over his birthright first. Esau was so hungry he agreed. Esau gave up his birthright for one meal!

In those days a birthright meant a double portion of his inheritance, which is due the eldest child. Both men were wrong. Esau had no patience and foolishly gave up something of tremendous value for something of little value that only lasted a short time. And Jacob manipulated his brother to get something of great value but sacrificed his relationship with his brother to do so, as Esau swore to take vengeance on his brother later. But is this really so hard to believe that Esau gave up so much for just one short moment to get what he wanted? We do things like this all the time in today's age. We may want to go somewhere and our parents say no, so we sneak out of the house, get in trouble, and terrible things can result. Or we are curious about what it would be like to experiment with a drug or alcohol, and the consequence can be deadly even. Remember today's message, "when you think you can't wait, think twice."

Let's pray, "Lord, thank you for giving us our minds to be able to think things through when we have tough choices and decisions to make. We ask that you give us the patience and recognition during a decision time to come to you in prayer for guidance first. Then we can trust that whatever happens from there you will help make it right and help us through any difficulties that result."

WHO WROTE THE BOOKS OF THE NEW TESTAMENT?

I know many of you have the books of the bible memorized. We may have favorite passages we have memorized from certain books of the bible. But have you ever wondered who wrote each of the books and to whom they wrote them? This is actually important historical information because many skeptics and non-believers often say that we do not know who the authors of the bible are so how can we believe it? But for the most part, this criticism is not true. Even though some books do not indicate within who the author is, the early Christian leaders knew and recorded it in their own writings. So we must use a combination of historical proof but also oral tradition. There is no reason not to believe them. And it is important for you to know more about these authors and their purposes.

Today let's take a look at some of the books of the NT and see who wrote them and who they wrote them to. See how many you know.

BOOK	AUTHOR	WHO HE WAS	WHO HE WROTE IT TO AND PURPOSE	DATE
Matthew	Anonymous, but church tradition says Matthew	Levi the tax collector, apostle	To Jews to show Jesus was Messiah	AD 60's
Mark	Anonymous but church tradition says Mark	Also known as John Mark, disciple of the 12, Peter's assistant	To Jews to show Jesus was the suffering Son of God	AD 60, thought to be the earliest written of the gospels
Luke	Anonymous but church tradition says Luke	Doctor, not a disciple, Paul's assistant and companion	Wrote it for Paul while Paul was under arrest. Luke interviewed all the eyewitnesses of the miracles and resurrection. Wrote about Jesus as Savior for Jews but also Gentiles. Love your neighbor became important theme, and also emphasized Holy Spirit and prayer.	Prior to AD 62 because in Acts, it ends with Paul in prison but alive. We know Paul died in AD 62
John	Anonymous but church tradition says John	Apostle, the one Jesus loved. Only apostle not martyred.	Written for all. Emphasized the deity of Jesus. Jesus was the Word. The Word was God.	AD 90's
Acts	Luke	Paul's assistant	Gentiles. Written for everyone.	AD 60's
Romans	Paul	Apostle	Gentiles. Written to Christians in Rome.	AD 57
1 Corinthians	Paul	Apostle	Christians in Corinth	AD 54
2 Corinthians	Paul	Apostle	Christians in Corinth	AD later 50's
Galatians	Paul	Apostle	Christians in Galatia	AD early 50's
Ephesians	Paul	Apostle	Christians in Ephesus	AD early 60's

DON'T HAVE A COW	
Scripture verses	Exodus 32:1-35
High level key topic	God is patient with us

SCRIPTURAL LESSON NARRATIVE

The theme this month is patience. Patience is when you wait for something that you want now. When you realize you are about to be impatient, remember how patient God is with us. He waits for us to obey and although He may test us or discipline us, God never gives up on us. So we should also be patient with others. When you feel you are about to be impatient, pray to God and ask for help to be patient. He will guide your next steps. If you forget and lose your patience, pray to God and ask forgiveness and help, strength and the will power to control yourself the next time.

In today's story, the Israelites were so impatient they could not wait more than 40 days while Moses went up to Mt. Sinai to receive the Ten Commandments. They doubted he was coming back and thought something happened to him. So in the meantime, Moses' brother Aaron was in charge and the people demanded he help them make a god to worship. So they gave him all their gold jewelry and he put it in a fire and a gold calf was made. God told Moses what was going on and that he must punish the people but he agreed to not destroy them all. When Moses returned he took the ones who still loved God and had them go through the people and destroy 3000 of those who were wicked. Then he burned the calf and threw the ashes over water and made the rest of the people drink it. Then a plague was sent on the rest of them but God did not destroy them all and forgave them and helped them build a nation from that point on.

This is a tough lesson. God is always righteous and does not do evil. So even though he commanded Moses to destroy people it was for the better for all those left or they would never turn away from worshiping other gods and would always be evil. So, sometimes God has to deliver judgment. Remember he destroyed those who were evil during Noah's time when he sent the flood also. And he commanded the Israelites to wipe out the Canaanites later on in the OT and to take over their land. But that is because the Canaanites were evil for 400 years and never repented. They were making child sacrifices and other evil all that time. If God had not had them destroyed, the Israelites would have married some of them and raised families that were evil and it would have continued. Sometimes God must deliver tough decisions and judgments. But His judgment is always righteous.

Let's pray, "Lord, thank you for giving us your word to see examples of how we should act or not act. Help us to be patient during difficult circumstances and think about how patient you are with us. Give us the will power and the courage to do the right thing. Amen."

WHO WROTE THE BOOKS OF THE NEW TESTAMENT?
PART 2

Many critics and non-believers say that we don't know the authors of the books of the bible; so why should we believe what is said? It is important for Christians to not only memorize the books but understand who wrote them, when, to whom, and the purpose

Today let's take a look at the next books of the NT.

BOOK	AUTHOR	WHO HE WAS	WHO HE WROTE IT TO AND PURPOSE	DATE
Acts	Not mentioned but oral tradition says Luke	Doctor, Paul's travelling companion & assistant	Unite Jews and Gentiles who were arguing, Acts of the apostles, history of early church. It's a historical account	Early AD 0's. Paul is in prison at end and he was beheaded in AD 63.
Romans	Paul, while in Corinth on 3rd missionary journey.	Apostle	Written to some 26 Romans friends/Christians who he hoped to visit. Written to explain salvation.	AD 57
1 Corinthians	Paul	Apostle	Written to members of Corinth church who were having problems such as wisdom, sacrifices, behavior and resurrection of the body.	AD 54
2 Corinthians	Paul. Technically this was his fourth letter to Corinth but the second and third were lost still, but mentioned in this letter.	Apostle	Paul sent Timothy to resolve the problems but it didn't work. So he himself went. After he visited Corinth because of bad reports, he wrote them a severe letter of correction. Then he journeyed to Macedonia and when he heard the report of his third letter, wrote this 4th letter. He asked them to get it together before he came for his next visit.	AD late 60's
Galatians	Paul	Apostle	Written to members of 4 churches in Galatia (Turkey). Urged them to only accept the true gospel and not false accounts.	AD 49 Probably the first letter he wrote.
Ephesians	Paul, but disputed, maybe written for him by a scribe. Written while he was in prison.	Apostle	Written to a large group of churches. May have been verification that his disciple Tychicus would tell them his message. Letter talks about the benefits and responsibilities of Christians.	AD late 50's or early 60's

THE PASSION OF CHRIST

Scripture verses	Matthew 26:36; 27
High level key topic	Christ sacrificed Himself to pay the penalty for our sins. Because He died for us we should live for Him

SCRIPTURAL LESSON NARRATIVE

Today's lesson is about what is often called the passion of Christ; the suffering He endured to bear the burden of our sins so that we might be saved and have eternal life when we accept Him as Lord and Savior of our lives.

All four gospels contain the story of Jesus' arrest, suffering and death on the cross. Critics and non-believers say the stories are not accurate because they don't all have the same details. But this is the way eyewitness reporting is in real life. No eyewitness recalls every detail the same way and may emphasize some and leave out others. That is the way it is written in the gospels. For example, the gospel of John does not even mention the flogging of Jesus. John writes mainly to emphasize that Jesus is the Son of God. Matthew wrote mainly for the Jewish audience and so he emphasized many more details that would be important for a Jew to hear and understand. But we can be sure that each gospel author had his own reasons for what he described and that collectively we have the full story and it is all true. Some critics and Muslims in particular deny that Jesus even died on the cross. They say it was either a replacement because God would not allow His son to die or that He survived. In either case they say there was no resurrection because Jesus did not die. Is this even believable? We will look at the evidence.

The key points to remember about the crucifixion;

- Jesus gave Himself up willingly to fulfill the Father's plan for our salvation

- Jesus was/is God.

- Jesus did die and was resurrected and is alive now in heaven as we speak.

- Although Jesus died to save everyone, we can only be saved to eternal life if we ask forgiveness of our sins and accept Jesus as Lord and Savior.

- Because Jesus died to save each one of us we should make Him the focal point of our lives and follow His commands.

- This life is a preparation for the life to come. If we live our lives by following Jesus' commands and serving Him and others, it will help make us ready for the amazing experience we will have in heaven one day.

WHO WROTE THE BOOKS OF THE NEW TESTAMENT?

The evidence is really overwhelming so it is hard to understand anyone would deny it except based on bias and personal beliefs.

1. It was predicted that the Messiah would die (Psalms, Isaiah, Daniel, and Zechariah). Jesus fulfilled this prediction and 100 others that prove He was the Messiah.

2. Jesus predicted His own death (all gospels – Matt 17:22-23 specifically)

3. Historically, virtually all bible scholars, Christian and non-Christian, except for Muslims, agree that Jesus died on the cross.

4. Nature of injuries and crucifixion

   a. No sleep the night before

   b. Beaten and whipped

   c. Collapsed carrying the cross

   d. Roman executioners knew how to kill and determine if someone was dead. Their lives depended on it.

   e. They declared Him dead and did not break His legs

   f. There were eyewitnesses to His death

   g. The spear piercing resulted in blood and water (serum forms around heart after death

   h. No one ever survived a crucifixion

   i. He hung on the cross bleeding from 9 AM to sunset

   j. Ongoing pain of lifting up to breathe

   k. Modern medical doctors and coroners state the evidence shows He was dead

l. Scripture says it was His last breath and He says He was giving Himself up

m. Pilate double checked He was dead before He gave the body to Joseph of Arimathea

n. Jesus wrapped in 75 pounds of cloth and spices in damp tomb for three days with no medical treatment, food or water

o. Several non-Christian sources from the first and second century wrote that He died

p. Earliest Christian writers all wrote that He died for our sins

5. The disciples all believed He died and met to talk about what to do next

FAITH	
Scripture verses	Hebrews 12:1, 11
High level key topic	Faith is the hope of what is unseen. We don't need blind faith. We can believe because of what He has made and done.

SCRIPTURAL LESSON NARRATIVE

Faith is a misunderstood word in today's world. Critics and nonbelievers think Christians are foolish to believe in something they cannot see. They think that is blind faith and irrational. But you cannot see the wind or your consciousness yet they exist. Faith is the hope in what is unseen because of what we can see. We can see the amazing world God has made and believe He did it. We can read the Word of God in the Bible and believe because we know the Bible is reliable and actually is a record of history.

So blind faith is not what Christians need. There is a point where there is no sufficient proof to be 100% certain of anything and therefore there is some measure of faith you must have. And the Bible tells us we cannot have salvation without faith. But very few, if any, things in the world have 100% certainty. But that doesn't mean we don't still believe in them. We know that accidents occur every day but we have enough faith to believe we will make it through the day instead of staying indoors in fear. When we get in an elevator, we have enough faith to believe it will work; the same with an airplane or a car. But none of those are 100% certain.

The Christian faith contains significant evidence to provide belief in it, God, Jesus, and the Bible. One of the reasons God and Jesus performed miracles was to help the people believe.

So don't fall for anyone telling you it is silly to believe in something you cannot see. The universe is here and no one saw it begin. Life exists and no one saw it begin. But we see the effects of it all and can have faith and believe it happened.

Today's scripture discusses Paul's explanation of faith and many of the OT patriarchs who had faith. Let's read first Hebrews 12:1, then Hebrews 11. Then let's pray that we remember these verses in times of trouble and allow them to help support and guide us when we face difficulties and need to have faith.

WAS JESUS REALLY RESURRECTED?

One of the most important and best evidences we have for Christianity is actually the resurrection of Jesus. But many who deny miracles are possible refuse to believe it even though the evidence is convincing. And other religions such as Islam in particular, deny that Jesus even died so they say there was no resurrection. Let's look at the minimal facts case for the resurrection. The "minimal facts" approach relies on presentation only of evidence that is strong; and second, that virtually all scholars on the subject, even skeptic scholars, grant each of the pieces of data.

1. JESUS DIED BY CRUCIFIXION

Reported in all four gospels by four different authors, and 5 non-Christian sources: Josephus, a well-known Jewish historian of the time; Tacitus, a Roman senator and historian; Lucian, a Greek satirist; Mara Bar-Serapion, a Stoic philosopher from Syria; and the Talmud, a Rabbinic Jewish text. In fact, John Domonic Crossan, the very critical scholar from the Jewish Seminar (not exactly an evangelical) said "That he was crucified is as sure as anything historical can ever be."

2. JESUS' DISCIPLES BELIEVED HE ROSE AND APPEARED TO THEM

The disciples claimed it themselves, and then transformed into aggressive preachers of the gospel to the point of martyrdom for all of them save John, who likely died on the Isle of Patmos. The Apostle Paul claimed it as well via the oral tradition recorded in the early creed, expressed in 1 Corinthians 15:3-8. The amazing change in the disciples' behavior is phenomenal in its own right as they had previously proven to be timid, even cowards when they scattered upon Jesus' arrest and disappeared during the crucifixion and denied knowing him. Once they believed they saw him, everything changed and they were courageous, dauntless and aggressive in spite of imprisonment, beatings, torture and execution. No one would put themselves through that for a lie unless they fully believed it. Seven ancient sources confirm that the apostles claimed they saw the Resurrected Jesus.

As for any claims of people who don't believe the Bible, you can take the theology out of it for this piece of evidence and merely accept the historicity of the gospels, which again, even skeptical scholars confirm.

3. THE APOSTLE PAUL'S TRANSFORMATIONN

He transformed from a major persecutor of the church into the Apostle Paul, one of the greatest messengers of the gospel of all time. What could possibly account for this? It was his encounter with the Resurrected Jesus, about two years later, while travelling on the road to Damascus where he had orders to pick up Christians and take them back to Jerusalem for imprisonment. His subsequent preaching, suffering and martyrdom are attested in his church letters and by Luke, his assistant; Clement of Rome; Polycarp; Tertullian; Dionysius of Corinth and Origen, all well-known figures of the time.

4. JAMES, BROTHER OF JESUS, ALSO TRANSFORMED

James was one of Jesus' brothers and sisters, reported in the gospels and by Jewish historian Josephus. James was not a believer or follower of Jesus, as documented in the gospels, prior to Jesus' resurrection. Along with Jesus' mother Mary, the Bible indicates (Mark 3:21, 31; 6:3-4; John 7:5) they thought Jesus to be mad and feared for his life at times. James is mentioned in the early creed of 1 Corinthians 15: 3-8 which states he was among those who saw the resurrected Jesus. After his witness of the Resurrected Jesus, he became a leader of the Jerusalem church (Acts 15:12-21; Galatians 1:19). Eventually James also died of martyrdom, attested by Josephus, Hegesippus and Clement of Alexandria.

Additionally: Three-quarters of scholars do accept the empty tomb as evidence. Resurrection is the most logical explanation for the empty tomb. The very fact that Romans claimed Jesus' body was stolen is evidence that the tomb was empty. In fact, scripture documents the Jewish leaders were concerned the disciples might steal the body and requested guard support at the tomb, and were granted the request.

Other fine points. It was unlikely that a Jewish Sanhedrin member (Jewish religious council) would be invented and named as the person who requested Jesus' body, then arrange the burial tomb. Clearly he was well-known in the community and this story could easily be checked out for falsification. Nothing like that happened.

Women were the first to discover the empty tomb. Since women's testimony was not allowed in a court of law, it is quite unlikely this story was invented.

Finally, no natural alternative explanation for the minimal facts has found to be more reasonable than those I shared. Some say hallucinations or wild animals ate the body, or Jesus didn't really die and was somehow healed, or Barabbas was killed, not Jesus. But there is no evidence for any of these.

Remember also the overall purpose of Jesus' life was to be a sacrifice for us because of the fall and because we cannot save ourselves from sin.

The evidence is too compelling not to believe. Even the most critical bible scholar of the NT agrees with all the evidence but refuses to believe it happened because he doesn't believe miracles are possible. He says that animals ate the body instead. But there is no historical fact or story that discusses that.

If the resurrection happened, it means Christianity is true. And that means it is critical for all people to take a knee and accept Christ as Savior. Amen.

April is a little scanty for lesson volume. This may be partly due to Easter holidays or travel or sickness. Utilize the extra lessons at the end if needed.

RISEN	
Scripture verses	Mark 16:5-7
High level key topic	God sacrificed His Son Jesus to pay the penalty for our sins. Because Jesus lives, we have salvation forever through Him if we believe and accept Him as Lord and Savior.

APOLOGETICS LESSON (DEFENDING CHRISTIANITY)

As the most important piece of evidence for Christianity, the Resurrection is due a repeat lesson. This time see if the kids can tell you what the evidence is in a competition.

THE EVIDENCE FOR THE RESURRECTION

One of the most important and best evidences we have for Christianity is actually the resurrection of Jesus. But many who deny miracles are possible refuse to believe it even though the evidence is convincing. And other religions such as Islam in particular, deny that Jesus even died so they say there was no resurrection. Let's look at the case for the resurrection.

Rather than get into the controversial evidence, let's look at what we call the minimal facts. The "minimal facts" approach relies on presentation only of evidence that is strong; and second, that virtually all scholars on the subject, even skeptic scholars, grant each of the pieces of data.

1. Jesus died by crucifixion

2. The crucifixion is reported in all four gospels by four different authors, and by 5 non-Christian sources: Josephus, a well-known Jewish historian of the time; Tacitus, a Roman senator and historian; Lucian, a Greek satirist; Mara Bar-Serapion, a Stoic philosopher from Syria; and the Talmud,

a Rabbinic Jewish text. In fact, John Domonic Crossan, the very critical scholar from the Jewish Seminar (not exactly an evangelical) said "That he was crucified is as sure as anything historical can ever be."

3. Jesus' disciples believed he rose and appeared to them

4. The disciples claimed it themselves, and then transformed into aggressive preachers of the gospel to the point of martyrdom for all of them save John, who likely died on the Isle of Patmos. The Apostle Paul claimed it as well via the oral tradition recorded in the early creed, expressed in 1 Corinthians 15:3-8. The amazing change in the disciples' behavior is phenomenal in its own right as they had previously proven to be timid, even cowards when they scattered upon Jesus' arrest and disappeared during the crucifixion and denied knowing him. Once they believed they saw him, everything changed and they were courageous, dauntless and aggressive in spite of imprisonment, beatings, torture and execution. No one would put themselves through that for a lie unless they fully believed it. Seven ancient sources confirm that the apostles claimed they saw the Resurrected Jesus and were willing to suffer and die for their claims.

5. As for any claims of people who don't believe the Bible, you can take the theology out of it for this piece of evidence and merely accept the historicity of the gospels, which again, even skeptical scholars confirm. Even authorship is irrelevant to these minimal facts.

6. The Apostle Paul's transformation

7. He transformed from a major persecutor of the church into the Apostle Paul, one of the greatest messengers of the gospel of all time. What could possibly account for this? It was his encounter with the Resurrected Jesus, about two years later, while travelling on the road to Damascus where he had orders to pick up Christians and take them back to Jerusalem for imprisonment. His subsequent preaching, suffering and martyrdom are attested in his church letters and by Luke, his assistant; Clement of Rome; Polycarp; Tertullian; Dionysius of Corinth and Origen, all well-known figures of the time.

8. James, brother of Jesus, also transformed

9. James was one of Jesus' brothers and sisters, reported in the gospels and by Jewish historian Josephus. James was not a believer or follow-

er of Jesus, as documented in the gospels, prior to Jesus' resurrection. Along with Jesus' mother Mary, the Bible indicates (Mark 3:21, 31; 6:3-4; John 7:5) they thought Jesus to be mad and feared for his life at times. James is mentioned in the early creed of 1 Corinthians 15: 3-8 which states he was among those who saw the resurrected Jesus. After his witness of the Resurrected Jesus, he became a leader of the Jerusalem church (Acts 15:12-21; Galatians 1:19). Eventually James also died of martyrdom, attested by Josephus, Hegesippus and Clement of Alexandria.

Additionally: Three-quarters of scholars do accept the empty tomb as evidence. It is the most logical explanation for the empty tomb. The very fact that Romans claimed Jesus' body was stolen is evidence that the tomb was empty. In fact, scripture documents the Jewish leaders were concerned the disciples might steal the body and requested guard support at the tomb, and were granted the request.

Other fine points. It was unlikely that a Jewish Sanhedrin member (Jewish religious council) would be invented and named as the person who requested Jesus' body, then arrange the burial tomb. Clearly he was well-known in the community and this story could easily be checked out for falsification. Nothing like that happened.

Women were the first to discover the empty tomb. Since women's testimony was not allowed in a court of law, it is quite unlikely this story was invented.

Finally, no natural alternative explanation for the minimal facts has found to be more reasonable than those I shared. Some say hallucinations or wild animals ate the body, or Jesus didn't really die and was somehow healed, or Barabbas was killed, not Jesus. But there is no evidence for any of these.

Remember also the overall purpose of Jesus' life was to be a sacrifice for us because of the fall and because we cannot save ourselves from sin.

The evidence is too compelling not to believe. Even the most critical bible scholar of the NT agrees with all the evidence but refuses to believe it happened because he doesn't believe miracles are possible. He says that animals ate the body instead. But there is no historical fact or story that discusses that.

If the resurrection happened, it means Christianity is true. And that means it is critical for all people to take a knee and accept Christ as Savior. Amen.

THE VISIT	
Scripture verses	Luke 24:13-35
High level key topic	Jesus was bodily resurrected and seen a dozen times by hundreds of people

SCRIPTURAL LESSON NARRATIVE

After the women found the empty tomb, then encountered Jesus, they went back and told all the disciples. Many did not believe. Peter made his own trip to the tomb and found it empty and was amazed and joyful.

Later that day, word had spread throughout Jerusalem about the events of the weekend. Two of the disciples who also went and found the tomb empty were travelling home to Emmaus, a small town about seven miles from Jerusalem, talking about everything that had happened. Suddenly Jesus appeared and began walking with them, but they were prevented from recognizing Him. He asked them what they were talking about and they were amazed He had not heard that the Jesus had been crucified, died, and buried but that very morning His tomb was found empty.

Jesus scolded them a little for being dull and slow and not realizing that the scriptures had prophesied all of these events. Jesus then proceeded to teach them about all the scriptures that foretold this. When they reached Emmaus, the disciples asked Jesus to come in with them for dinner. He did so and when He broke bread with them they suddenly recognized Him. But then He disappeared. The disciples were amazed and told each other how wonderful it was that He had spoken to them and taught them everything and how it had set their hearts on fire for Him. Then they walked back to Jerusalem yet that night and told all the disciples what had happened.

You can be sure that Jesus is risen and alive even today. His spirit is within you because you have accepted Him as your Savior. Pray now and thank Jesus again for what He has done and ask Him to guide you to find the path He has made for your life. Until you are with Him again in heaven, He lives within your heart. Be mindful of that in all that you do and be obedient to His teachings.

WAS JESUS RESURRECTED IN BODY OR SPIRIT?

Some critics refuse to believe that Jesus was resurrected bodily but rather believe it was only His spirit. Jehovah's Witnesses are one example. If it was only His spirit, it takes away from the actual historical record and distorts the idea that Jesus was not only God but also human. How do we know His resurrection was in a bodily form?

The New Testament is clear on this. You would have to completely ignore numerous references that prove Jesus had a bodily form when He arose. He ate and drank with disciples. He had Thomas touch his wounds. The women kissed His feet. Many people saw Him eat and drink.

Take a look at the chart below and see the order of appearances by Jesus and what took place.

APPEARANCE	MATTHEW	MARK	LUKE	JOHN	ACTS	I COR
Mary Magdalene		X		X		
Mary & Women	X	X				
Peter				X		X
Two disciples		X		X		
Ten apostles			X	X		
Eleven apostles				X		
Seven apostles				X		
All apostles (great commission)	X	X				X
500 brethren						X
James						X
All apostles (ascension)	X					
Paul					X	X

PERSEVERE	
Scripture verses	Hebrews 12:12-15
High level key topic	When life gets hard you can make it through and help others do the same

SCRIPTURAL LESSON NARRATIVE

Perseverance is an important quality or characteristic to learn. It means to not give up when things get hard. Life has challenges and difficulties for everyone. There will be times when you experience pain and sorrow and feel hurt, sometimes physically, and the same for your family and friends. But it will not last forever. You have to learn to be prepared for it and how to get through it.

Why does it happen to everyone, even good people? Sometimes it is because others make poor decisions or maybe you make a poor decision and it has consequences. Sometimes it is just bad luck. Sometimes things happen for a reason God planned; for a lesson to be learned. But God does not deceive or cause you harm although He may test your faith. But when something bad happens don't blame God for it. Believe in Him and that He has a plan for this difficulty which will help you somehow and turn it into something good for you. Maybe you will become a strong person because of the difficulty. Maybe it will teach you how to help others through difficulties. Maybe it will bring you into the path of some person that God has planned who will make a difference in your life or you will in their life. Perhaps you have a sin that you refuse to give up like pride or seeking some idol that is more important than God. God may teach you that it is wrong by disciplining you. But God does not directly cause harm to you or inflict pain and hurt in you in a physical way.

We have talked before about how evil and suffering is in the world and everyone experiences it. But there are benefits too: you learn to get through hard times; help others get through hard times; teaches you compassion; brings you closer to God and to realize you can't manage your life without Him.

So when difficult times come, be ready. Trust in God. Pray and ask Him for strength and to guide you through the difficulty. Praise Him for the opportunity to show you still trust Him in your difficulty. You can even thank Him for the problem because you know He already has a plan to turn it into something good for you.

THE TRINITY

We have talked about how we have evidence to show that God exists, that the Bible is true, and that Jesus was resurrected. Those explanations are done by evidence. But what about the Trinity, one of the most important Christian fundamentals of our faith? It is an extremely difficult concept and mainly a mystery to be accepted by faith alone. No one but a Christian believes God is one essence in three persons. Not three Gods but one nature with three individual persons that are God. But there are some ways to explain it to some degree for a basic understanding.

The fact that the Son, the second person of the Trinity, was only fully revealed in the NT when Jesus arrived creates a lot of the confusion.

First, where does scripture tell us that the Father, Son and Holy Spirit are all God?

1. Scriptural basis

    a. Deut. 6:4 – the lord our God is one (shema)

    b. Father is God – Gal. 1:1 – I am

    c. Son is God – John 8:58, 10:30, Col. 2:9

    d. I and the Father are one – they tried to stone him then

    e. HS is God – Acts 5:3-4 you have not lied to men but to God, as he described the HS

    f. Divine persons distinct – Matt. 3:16 – this is my beloved Son...

    g. Matt. 28:19 make disciples...

How do we try to understand the Trinity? Well, one of the great early church leaders, Thomas Aquinas, explained it this way:

You know what consciousness is right? Close your eyes and think for a minute and envision who you are. Think of the person that is you. This is the way Aquinas describes the concept of the Trinity.

God the Father loves Himself and has an image of Himself. This image can be said to be the Son. So God also loves the Son since it is Himself. The Son also loves the Father since they are the same. This love is the Holy Spirit, the spirit of love. So when the Son is born in human form, He contains the Holy Spirit, which is the love between the Father and Himself. But then the Son has the Father send the Holy Spirit also to each person when they accept Christ so that each of us has the spirit of love inside us, the Holy Spirit. All three are God but each has a different role. Yet each has all the attributes of God.

Now let's try to look at some examples, good and bad, that try to help us understand how God can have one nature and three persons:

Not the best ones:

1. 3 states of water

    a. No given drop of water is in all three states at the same time

        i. Modalism – a heresy; God does not become different persons at different times

2. 3 links in a chain

    a. The links are 3 different things – tritheism heresy (3 gods)

3. Human body, soul and spirit

    a. Body and soul separate at death but Godhead is always together – and God is pure spirit, no body

Better ones:

a. Triangle – three sides but all are equal angles and totally compose the triangle

b. One to the third power

c. Love is trifold – requires lover, beloved, and the spirit of love

d. Mind, ideas and words – each distinct but all of the same essence

These help a little but it is still very much a mystery how all that can actually be. So we believe the rest based on faith.

THE ASCENSION

Scripture verses	Acts 1:4-11
High level key topic	When life gets hard, you can make it through and help others do the same

SCRIPTURAL LESSON NARRATIVE

It's been 40 days after Jesus' resurrection. He appeared 11 times to over 500 people, including most of his original 11 disciples. Now His work is done and it is time to return to the Father's right hand and rule from heaven. But even after all that has happened the disciples still seem not to understand and ask Him if He will now take Israel back from Roman rule. Jesus says it is not for them to know but only for the Father.

Jesus asks the disciples to stay in Jerusalem and that they will receive the power of the Holy Spirit in a few days. That power will enable them to do wonders and Jesus commands them to be His witnesses In Jerusalem, Judea, Samaria and the ends of the earth.

Then Jesus is taken up into the clouds and disappears. But two angels appear to the disciples and explain He will one day return to earth just as He left.

The command to be His witnesses is not just for the disciples. It is also for us. Jesus wants us to learn everything about His teachings and then share it with others wherever we are and wherever we go. Will you try to do that and obey Him to show that you love Him? Pray about it and God will lead you.

WHEN WILL JESUS COME AGAIN?

The bible does not tell us when Jesus will return. Jesus does talk about some of the signs that will occur when the time is near. There will be great earthquakes, wars and rumors of wars, our moral values will be in decline, there will be an explosion of information in the world, and Israel will become a nation again after being scattered. The disciples thought His return would be very soon. Each generation since thinks He is coming soon. Even now many think His return is close.

There is still considerable debate about the order of events when He does return. There is the rapture belief as we call it, where Christians past and present meet up with Jesus in the clouds to be in heaven with Him before the great Tribulation period of 7 years during which the 7 seals, 7 trumpets and 7 bowls of God's judgment are delivered on the earth. As the time for Jesus's return is upon us, the final battled called Armageddon occurs where the world battles against Israel. But then Jesus returns in what we call His second coming, just in the nick of time and defeats all enemies to save Israel. He sends Satan and his demons into the pit in chains. This kicks off a period of 1000 years of Jesus' rule on earth. Christians return to earth to help Him rule over those who survived the tribulation. Then Satan is released for a short period of time to tempt those left. But after a short period of time, Satan and other demons and nonbelievers are put in the Lake of Fire for eternity. Then the New Jerusalem is formed; a vast area where we will all live with Jesus here on earth, perhaps just above the earth, forever. We will have bodies that do not wear down; there will be no pain or tears, no worry or fear, only joy and praise forever.

The order that those events occur is still in debate among bible scholars. The order I mentioned is the way most believe it occurs. Perhaps you can study and come to your own conclusion. Are you ready and prepared if this sequence of events kicked off tomorrow? No one knows the time or day when it will occur. Prepare yourself now; make sure you are solid in your faith in Jesus. Do not fear this time. Whatever pleasure we think we have now in the world, heaven and our time with Jesus will be wonderful in comparison.

MAY LESSONS

BE CONTENT	
Scripture verses	Philippians 4:11-13
High level key topic	When you focus on God, He can help you be content

SCRIPTURAL LESSON NARRATIVE

Content means you decide to be happy with what you have or with your situation. This is a hard lesson because we live in a world where we are taught to always compete and push ourselves to get more. So it seems like a contradiction at first. But you can still push yourself to be your best and still be content with whatever your circumstances are at the time. Don't stress over it.

Let's look at some verses that tell us about being content:

> John 16:33
>
> Psalm 139:14
>
> 1 Thessalonians 5:18
>
> Joshua 1:9
>
> 1 Samuel 16:7

Paul was a good example of how to be content. At the time he wrote some of the passages above he was in prison and physically beat up and had little food or water and no control over his situation. Yet he said he was content. He was not driving himself crazy trying to figure out what to do or how to survive. He just trusted in Christ to see Him through.

More importantly, knowing that He had Christ and would be with Him one day again and that He could count on God to help Him through any circumstance gave him peace and strength. This is the secret to being content. Focus on God. When you focus on God, you worry less about your own problems. Pray and put your fate in His hands and make it His problem to work out not yours.

Why is this important? If you are not content with your situation, sin more easily enters your life. You will start to feel envious of those who have more or something you don't have but want. You may feel jealous. You may learn to dislike others who have what you do not have. This leads to evil and may destroy your life. It may also make you resent God and blame Him that He doesn't give you more or what you want. We have this situation in our country today. Many people think that the country and government owes them things. That the government should pay for our entire healthcare, our education, give us a job or pay us if we don't have a job. They want the government to be responsible for their lives instead of themselves.

And what if God has a reason that He has not given you what you want or changed your circumstance? When you complain or become envious and want more that is you trying to take control of your life and your plan. But what if God has a reason for preventing you from getting what you want? What if it is for your own good because He loves you? What if He has a lesson for you to learn in your current situation or what if what you want will somehow hurt you or others or cause a disaster? Should you trust God or trust yourself?

Trust God. Focus on God. Always try to do your best but be content with what you have and trust that God knows how to complete the plan for your life better than you.

What situations have you struggled with in your life where you were not content or chose to be content with your situation?

WHAT IS NECESSARY FOR SALVATION?

Salvation should be the goal for every person. What is it? Salvation is living with God forever, even after we pass this world into the next. But it is often misunderstood and sometimes confusing how to achieve it and how it works. Let's look at that.

First, how do we achieve it? There is no single verse in the bible that tells us. There is John 3:16 which is often used. But that doesn't say anything about asking to be forgiven for sins, and also, demons believe Jesus is God but they are not saved. Another is Romans 10:13 but that also misses the part where we ask forgiveness of our sins. We were taught the ABCs of salvation earlier in our children's Sunday school. Admit you are a sinner; believe that Jesus is God; confess He is your Savior and Lord. These are the basic elements and have been strung together to help us. Has everyone said that type of prayer to be saved through Christ and sincerely believe?

How does the actual salvation process work? What about people who are learning about God or seeking God or thinking about God or have rejected God and are still not saved? How can they be saved?

The combination of the Father, the Son and the Holy Spirit, as well as the individual, all play key roles in salvation. Remember that in our lesson last week we learned the persons of the Trinity are all God but exist in different persons for different purposes. The Father planned for our salvation; Christ achieved our salvation opportunity through His sacrifice for our sins; the Holy Spirit finalizes and applies our salvation for us when it is known that we are about to accept Jesus. Let's take a closer look.

For those who are not yet saved, at some point they may reject the gospel and not reject their sin. But when they become seekers and begin to learn about Christ they may move to a position where eventually they stop rejecting the gospel and stop accepting their sin. Now these two are in perfect opposition but they are not yet saved. We call this a state of 'quiescence'. We have not yet accepted the gospel but cannot accept our sin any longer. It is at this point that God gives this person some measure of grace; perhaps this is the beginning of what we call faith. Then with this measure of grace the person is able to accept the gospel, reject their sin and become saved. The Holy Spirit helps that last part become final.

For those who still refuse to accept the gospel and reject their sin, they will live with their sin forever and be separated from God. God sacrificed Himself for all but it is up to each person to make their decision to believe that and accept Christ as Savior. If they cannot, God does not accept them into heaven. We each choose our final destiny. Rather than think of God as banishing someone to hell, understand that each person decides what their fate will be. They have to take responsibility and not blame God.

DO NOT COVET

Scripture verses	1 Kings 21: 1-28
High level key topic	Don't desire what others have

SCRIPTURAL LESSON NARRATIVE

Last week we talked about being content; be happy with what you have. We discussed that it is fine and good to seek to improve yourself and your situation but that until that happens be okay with where you are. There may be some lesson to learn before you move up to the next level of whatever you seek. To ignore that may be to ignore God's plan and you may try to obtain something that God was not ready for you to have. So work hard to improve yourself but don't stress over it if things don't go your way and you get stuck in a situation where you feel unhappy. Be content and find joy in the Lord no matter what good or bad befalls you.

Today's lesson goes one step further. Do not see what another person has and want it for yourself. That is what we call covet. It involves a type of jealousy and envy and worse; the desire to take something from someone else so that it can be yours instead.

Today's scripture is a sad lesson about an evil king in the Old Testament who did just that. Read 1 Kings 21:1-28. It demonstrates how much God dislikes it when we covet. But it also demonstrates God's forgiveness when we repent from our sins.

Probably in your own life you may have friends who live in a bigger house with a pool or have a fancier car or bike than you or better clothes or money to go on cool vacations and outings. It's okay to hope for things like that for yourself but until it happens or if it doesn't happen be happy where you are. You may have the more loving parents and family and better relationship with Christ so that is more important. And don't want someone else's material thing to be yours. That is when you begin to covet. It is a sin and leads to other sins like resentment, jealousy and complaining and pretty soon you are unhappy and questioning why God does not give you similar things.

Remember, whatever your situation, it could always be much worse than it is. Be happy that God has blessed you with what you have and remember to thank Him every day for it because it can be taken away in an instant. Then you will be thinking, if only I had what I used to have.

PRAYER

Prayer is one of the most important parts of being a Christian. If you do not pray to God regularly, you are not in synch with Him. You will not feel His presence and will not hear His advice and feel His guidance by the Holy Spirit. Prayer can help you feel close to God, feel at peace with difficulties in your life when they happen, and help show your faith in God. Of course He already knows what you are thinking and feeling so prayer is not for God it is for us. It helps us deal with our world and our situation.

When and where and how and how often should we pray? As much as you can wherever you are. A prayer can be as simple as "Help me Jesus" or "I trust you Jesus". Or it can be longer. It can be for you or for another or just a talk with God about things that are on your mind.

Sometimes when you pray for something specific you may want an immediate answer. Sometimes God will give it to you and sometimes not. Sometimes He has something better in mind for you and you may not find out how He answered your prayer until much later or maybe you will never realize it. But you can trust that He heard your prayer and answered it in the way that was best for you. He knows everything and knows what is best for you.

Sometimes you should have a longer prayer that includes asking forgiveness for your mistakes and sins, thanking God for everything and everyone you have in your life, telling Him what is in your mind that is bothering you or just talking to God about whatever is on your mind.

Don't ever think it is too late to make a prayer. I have a couple examples from my own life that include a miracle and another that gave me great hope. Two of the elements of prayer to understand are that God is omniscient; he knows everything; and He is eternal. He knows the entire past, present and future. How might this impact our prayer? Let me give you a couple examples from my own life and from my studies about God;

- An email came into my inbox that I had been waiting for. It was from an important potential client and I couldn't help but fear bad news. Is it too late to pray and ask God to help it be good news? One might think so because it is already in your inbox so it wouldn't make sense that God would change the wording suddenly and that the person who sent it either wouldn't know or would not remember. But that is not even necessary. God knows everything and is everywhere in past, present and future and existed before time began. God knew before He even created the heavens and earth and you that you would make that prayer at exactly that time. So that means God could have created and influenced the right circumstances for the email to say something good or maybe even better than you hoped. He didn't have to change anything. But if you had not made that prayer at the last second, maybe it would not have happened. Now that doesn't mean that God will answer every prayer as you hope. This is just an example to show it is never too late to pray.

- Here's another one I have been thinking about and praying for lately. It has to do with my dad's salvation. My father passed over 40 years ago. I never knew if He was saved but always had the idea that he was not because he never went to church or talked about God and none of my relatives could confirm that he believed in God. So it has been something that has bothered me for a long, long time. I just thought since he had passed away 40 years ago that there was nothing I could do now. Once a person is gone it is too late for them to make a decision for Christ and after death God does not provide salvation and change the situation just because you pray for them. Each person has to make their own decision. But a few years ago something happened. I found some very old letters from my father that no one knew about. In them he mentioned God a number of times. And my father had a strong character and integrity and lived a good life although we know that is not what gets you into heaven. But I began to think because he mentioned God in the letters a few times that maybe he actually believed and I never knew it. I started praying regularly to God that it be true and that somehow and somewhere in his life he believed in God enough to receive salvation. But until recently, it never occurred to me that my prayers could have any impact on something that happened over 40 years ago. Now, think about this: what if my prayers now were known to God before creation and that because of my prayers and my father's acknowledging God to some degree that God provided the right influence and circumstances for my dad to be saved after all? But maybe without my prayers it would not have happened? I have no way of knowing if that is the case. But it gives me hope for Him and it is certainly possible.

- A serious tax issue that God resolved with an immediate miracle. Let's net this out and say earlier this year I talked with an expert tax accountant and was told my business had a $100,000 tax liability from last year and another for this year and that in a week we were supposed to pay $45,000 at a minimum. But we couldn't pay it. I got off the phone and prayed to God to help us through this or even better, to find a solution so we didn't have to owe it. Then I called my partner and discussed it and he could tell I was very stressed and worried about it. While on the phone he said let's find another accountant and he sent out emails to about 100 accountants in the southeast and one actually responded before our call ended and we scheduled a phone appointment with him the next day. He was sympathetic, brilliant, and came up with an incredibly creative idea on how to restructure our company legally and make the tax liability go away. Not only did we end up not having to pay anything but he did my personal taxes also and generated a substantial refund for me. Our total cost to him was $250 for our business tax return and $150 for my personal return. If not for him, we would have had to declare bankruptcy. But when it happened I immediately recognized this was a miracle from God and that in this case He answered my prayer specifically the way I asked and created an even better result than I could have ever hoped for.

- A false positive test for cancer that was a great relief

- My aunts and uncle and sister that God sustains at ages 104, 100, 96 and 76.

There is no logical limit to the power of prayer and the power of God. Never underestimate it and never feel it is too late to pray for something. But once you pray, trust in God to take it from there and be content with whatever happens from that point.

DON'T LOOK BACK	
Scripture verses	Exodus 16:2-21, 17:1-4
High level key topic	Don't focus on the past or you may miss something important in the present

SCRIPTURAL LESSON NARRATIVE

The older you get, the more experiences you will have. Sometimes we tend to think back when we liked our situation better and wish we had it again. You might complain that things were better then. Maybe you used to have a nicer house or more friends or a better job than now. But when you focus on looking back you may miss out on what is right in front of you. Maybe your new best friend is sitting next to you in school and you are thinking so much about how you lost your old friends that you never say hi to your neighbor and perhaps miss out on an even better friend.

When you look back, you may miss what is right in front of you. And worse, it is a type of rebellion and complaint to God as though you are saying, "No God, I want the old situation." But that is trying to take control of your life's plan away from God. Try to realize that God has your plan in His hands and that if you try to complain and not follow it you will be fighting against God. So we should accept our circumstances as they are. Now that does not mean we can't think about the past and have good memories of some things and we can learn from things in the past. But use that information to keep your eyes wide open for what is in front of you. Trust God. Wherever you are now and whatever is going on is in God's hands and He will deliver you through it and even provide something good for you. So instead of thinking about the past, pay attention to now and look for what God may be doing in your life.

Today's story is about the Israelites in the desert for 40 years after God directed Moses to free the people from Egypt and lead them to the Promised Land. But it took 40 years and it wasn't easy. Almost immediately when they encountered some difficulties the people grumbled and complained that they were better off being slaves in Egypt. At least they had a meal every day. It took a long time for them to learn to trust God in their new circumstances. But if they had not trusted Him and tried to go back they never would have reached the Promised Land and never would have created their own nation and prospered. Let's read the story and remember to focus on what is right in front of you and what God might be doing in your life now instead of complaining about wanting things to be the way they used to be.

JUSTICE vs MERCY

God is all just and all merciful. In other words, He delivers justice but also provides mercy. Justice is giving people what they rightly deserve. Mercy is giving someone forgiveness that they don't deserve.

So some critics of Christianity will say this is a contradiction and so they object to God as being both all just and all merciful. For example, if we are all sinners and deserve justice yet God provides mercy, some escape justice. How do we reconcile this seeming conflict?

First, God's mercy is delivered merely by the fact that He created us and gave us everything we need to be us; humans. We don't deserve existence but He provides it. Second, God's justice for sin is delivered in two ways: those who reject God will find eternal hell so justice is done for their sin; but for those who accept God, Jesus pays for the sins in your place and justice is still served.

God wants everyone to receive salvation and that is merciful. But not all do so is He unjust? No, because He loves us He gave us the freedom to choose to love Him back or reject Him so that is a decision people make that prevents everyone from being saved.

IS MORE BETTER	
Scripture verses	Luke 12:13-22
High level key topic	When you focus on stuff you miss what matters. Focus on serving God and others.

SCRIPTURAL LESSON NARRATIVE

Is bigger better? Is more better? Sometimes they are not. When we focus our lives on pursuit of material things, we often miss what matters most. God wants us to focus on Him and on loving and helping others. This is really our calling in life: to love God and help others. But many people get distracted by pursuit of money and wealth, position, power and material things. They spend all their time trying to store up more and more things but for what? When you leave this world you will leave with nothing just like you arrived with nothing. Instead of focus on the things of the world focus your time on God and others.

Today's story is a parable. Jesus used parables to teach lessons through story-telling. It relates a real-world situation to a heavenly lesson. The parable of the rich fool is not often studied. In it a rich man has so many goods and things that he wants to tear down all his barns to build bigger ones to stores his stuff. Then he says he can just sit around and drink and eat and enjoy himself. But God warns him that he may lose his life and then who will have the things he prepared? The Egyptians used to bury their kings with riches thinking they could take them along in the afterlife. But it doesn't work that way.

If you spend your life building up riches and storing them, you lose sight of what is in front of you – God and people who need your love and help. If you focus on worldly riches you will not be rich toward God. The story goes on later to explain that you demonstrate a lack of faith when you worry about your life too much and how you will take care of yourself. Jesus explained that the birds and flowers are taken care of by God so why would he not even more so take care of us, those made in His image? The idea of us selling our possessions and giving to the poor is not a command so don't worry too much. But it is encouragement for us to help others who are less fortunate than we are and a lesson to trust God and not worry about how much worldly things we have or do not have but to instead focus on Godly things.

WHY ALL THE BIBLE VERSIONS?

Have you ever wondered why there are so many different Bible versions and which one you should use? There are over 50 now. Critics of Christianity claim that all these different versions prove that the Bible has been changed and corrupted so much over the centuries that we can't trust it. Are they right? How should we understand why we have so many versions that say some of the verses using different words? And new versions come out all the time so should we be concerned about that?

To understand this problem first we have to remember in our lessons about Bible reliability that when we compare all the oldest manuscripts from Greek, Latin and other languages, the 5700 of them, they all agree in their writings to over 95% accuracy. So there is nothing to worry about. But why then all the versions?

Well, partly this has to do with keeping up with current language. For example, the King James Version reads like Shakespeare because it was developed in that age so people could understand the words better. When we changed a key word in John 3:16 from "begotten" to "one and only Son" we did not change the meaning but rather we omitted a word no one uses or understands anymore and replaced it with everyday language.

But actually, the different versions are much more than that. Let's take a look:

There are 4 main types of Bible translations:

Word for Word – King James Version, New American Standard Bible, and English Standard Version are examples.

- Scholars try to translate each word based on the word usage at the time of the writing.

Balance – New International Version, God's Word Translation are examples

- Scholars try to compromise between a word for word and thought for thought approach.

Thought for thought – New Living Translation, Contemporary English Version,

New International Reader's Version are examples

- Scholars translate the meanings of thoughts into modern English.

Paraphrase – The Message Version is an example.

- A restatement of the translation in modern terms, often expanded for clarity.

What's best? To answer this question you should determine if you are using it for serious study or simple daily reading.

Most pastors and teachers prefer a word for word version for their personal reading but recommend Balanced or Thought for Thought to those they teach as it is easier to understand.

If you are looking for a literal translation for study purposes, then word for word is better.

If one is new to Bible reading, a thought for thought might be better because it is easier to understand.

Technically, no version is truly word for word because the languages do not fully translate word for word. And you also have the issue that English has about 4 million words but Hebrew only has about 3000 and Greek about 5000 so many words have multiple meanings. Scholars have to get together and discuss how the word is being used and compare it to more common and frequent examples elsewhere in the Bible where the meaning is clear so they can determine which of its meanings is meant in a particular example.

Again, the important thing to remember is that this discussion is not about whether the Bible is reliable – it is. A comparison of all the thousands of manuscripts shows an amazingly high degree of accuracy. You can trust in the Bible.

JUNE LESSONS

GOD IS LOVE	
Scripture verses	1 John 4:10-12
High level key topic	God loved us so much He sacrificed His Son for us. So we should obey Him and also love others.

SCRIPTURAL LESSON NARRATIVE

What is love? God gave us the perfect example. He loved us so much that He was willing to lay down His Son's life to save us. Can there be any greater love than to give your life for another?

God is loving and is also love. God is actually love itself. Love comes from God and is part of His being. It is in the world because it is actually a piece of God. We can understand love because of the example of love that God showed us.

God is also the perfect example of love. Love is kind and forgiving. Love does not cause hurt. Love is gentle and caring. Love is putting others' needs and feelings ahead of your own. This is what Jesus did. It is what He wants us to do.

How can we show others we love them? Do things for them. Honor them. Respect them. Respond to their needs and requests. Find ways to show them we care.

Can you find it in your heart to love others just as Jesus loves you? If Jesus can love others, we can love them too.

WHAT DOES IT MEAN TO BE GOOD?

This is what Jesus asked the rich young ruler. "Why do you call me good?" He was testing the ruler to see if he really understood what good meant. Only God is good said Jesus. So good is an absolute standard represented by God. It cannot be arbitrary and subjective such that each of us has a different idea of what good is. Otherwise it creates anarchy. For one person good is anything we do except if we do physical harm to someone. For another it is okay for certain mild forms of physical harm but not something harsher. Everyone might have a different view. Society cannot function if everyone has their own view of what good is. This is actually one way we know that God exists. Where did this idea of good come from? It comes from God. You have to have a perfect standard to compare against in order to know if you fall short or meet it. There can only be one standard of perfect; not everyone's idea of what it is.

Good is the opposite of evil. Both are necessary in order to understand the other. Without good we cannot understand what evil is. If there were nothing but evil in the world, we would not recognize it as evil; we would think of it as normal. And if there were no evil in the world, we would not recognize it as good because it would just be normal.

God shows us through His word what it takes to be good. Only God can be perfectly good. But He reveals through his commands and laws enough for us to know right from wrong and good from evil.

Some critics of Christianity may say there is no God because an all-loving being would not allow evil, pain and suffering in the world. But if there is no God then where does good come from? We are not naturally good. We seek to serve ourselves. Only an understanding and desire for good keeps us from destroying ourselves and others and the entire world.

Don't be upset that evil exists. Without evil it is more difficult to see God and without evil we cannot know what good is.

PARABLES OF THE LOST SHEEP, COIN, SON

Scripture verses	Luke 15
High level key topic	God loved us so much He sacrificed His Son for us. So we should obey Him and also love others.

SCRIPTURAL LESSON NARRATIVE

Today's lesson is about 3 similar parables that Jesus taught. They came about because as he was starting to preach one day, many tax collectors and sinners sat down to listen to him but the Jewish religious leaders criticized Him, saying "Why does He meet with tax collectors and sinners?" So Jesus used the parables to explain the answer in a way that the religious leaders could not accept but the sinners would.

Jesus started with a lost sheep, saying if you have 100 sheep and one is lost, who would not search for the lost one while leaving the remaining ones where they were? Finding one lost sheep is like finding one sinner who repents. There is more joy in heaven when this happens than for people who have not repented. It signifies the importance of one being saved.

The Jesus explained a similar story about a woman with 10 coins who loses one and searches for it then calls her friends and family to celebrate with her when she finds it. Finally, a third parable is about a youngest son who asks his father for his inheritance then runs off and spends it all recklessly. He becomes so poor and desperate he works for nothing feeding pigs; hoping to get some of the seed pods they are eating because he is starving. He comes to his senses and realizes that even his father's servants eat better than that. So he decides to go back and ask his father's forgiveness and to be a servant. But when his father sees him, he welcomes him and has the servants prepare a feast because his son who was lost is now found. The oldest brother is upset and jealous about this, saying that he has never been so disrespectful and reckless but yet his father never had a feast for him. But the father says to not be upset but rejoice because your brother who was lost and dead is now found and alive.

The lessons are all about God's grace and the importance of salvation. We can't earn our way into heaven. Only as a gift do we enter. God continually seeks all of us to influence us to accept His gift of salvation through the Holy Spirit. When we do, all heaven sings praises of joy when a person repents and is saved.

IF GOD IS ALL GOOD, WHY DOES HE ALLOW EVIL?

For atheists (those who believe there is no God), this is the most frequently asked question. It is a difficult but important question. Here are several answers:

Evil came about because of sin. First Satan, then Eve and Adam sinned. This allowed evil to enter the world and to embed itself into every human person who descended from them. Also, God did not create evil. Evil is the absence of good. Further, because God allows humans free will to choose, they sometimes choose badly and that is sin. If God did not allow free will, we would all be robots and have no ability to make our own choices and that is not love. So God shows His love by allowing us to choose Him or to not choose Him.

Second, if there were no evil, we could not understand what good is. There would be no way to compare it. So evil, as horrible as it can be, provides us the understanding of what good is. We understand what love and compassion are only because we see what hate and insensitivity are. Knowing and experiencing evil, we learn to strive to be better and this builds our character. So evil actually helps us become better people.

Third, God does not make evil things happen. Some things happen in the world due to random chance and the laws of nature such as earthquakes, floods, disease and other disasters. Some of these came about because of the imperfections of sin and some happen in nature and God actually uses them for good. For example, as horrible as tornadoes and floods are when people are injured, killed, and driven from their homes, it provides the opportunity for others to show compassion and love.

Finally, although God has not destroyed evil yet, He will one day. The Bible says He will. After Jesus comes again, there will be a time when God ends all evil and throws the devil, his demons, and all those who have not accepted Jesus into the lake of fire forever. Then we will reign on earth with Jesus forever.

FRIENDS LOVE ONE ANOTHER

Scripture verses	1 John 4:11
High level key topic	Jesus loved us so we should love others

SCRIPTURAL LESSON NARRATIVE

What is love? The dictionary defines it as a great and tender affection for another person. But certainly there are different kinds of love. Can you give some examples?

Love is one of God's greatest gifts. It is to be given and received and shared with everyone at least in a Christian love sense. God loves everyone. We are not greater than God so we should also love everyone. Yet experiences and feelings sometimes get in the way and instead we dislike people or even resent and hate some people. This is not what God wants. We need to recognize that everyone is human and makes mistakes. Whatever it is we hold against them or that prevents us from loving them, we should let it go, turn it over to God and try to forgive them and find Christian love for them.

Paul defines love in 1 Corinthians 13:4-7. *Let's read it.* *4 Love is patient, love is kind. It does not envy, it does not boast, it is not proud.* *5 It does not dishonor others, it is not self-seeking, it is not easily angered, it keeps no record of wrongs.* *6 Love does not delight in evil but rejoices with the truth.* *7 It always protects, always trusts, always hopes, always perseveres.* So any feeling that does not contain those qualities or has the opposite qualities is not love. If you want to know if you love someone and are showing them love, use these verses as your guide.

WHAT IS HEAVEN LIKE?

Today we are going to start a lesson or two about heaven. What do you think heaven is like? What questions do you have about heaven? What does the Bible say about heaven?

No matter how much we may enjoy the current world, heaven will far surpass this world. And for those who don't like or trust this world, heaven will be like a dream come true. Let's examine some questions.

What does the Bible say about the end of the world?

What happens when we die?

Are there three heavens?

What is heaven?

Where is heaven?

Today let's explore scripture that helps us understand more about the new heavens and earth: the purpose, how we will recognize it, what it will be like:

Read Psalm 102:25-27

Read Mathew 5:18

Read Hebrews 12:26-27

Read Revelation 6:12-14

Read 2 Peter 3:10-12

Read Genesis 8:21-22

Read 2 Thessalonians 1:5-10

Read Joel 2:30-32

Read Revelation 2:10

Read Romans 8:19-22

Read Hebrews 10:16-17

Read 2 Peter 3:13

Read Mathew 24:29-31

Read 1 Thessalonians 416-17

Read 1 Corinthians 15:51-52

Read Revelation 11:15-17

Read 1 Corinthians 15:24

INTERCEDE	
Scripture verses	Acts 15:5-19
High level key topic	God wants us to care about others and pray for them

SCRIPTURAL LESSON NARRATIVE

This month our theme is about God. Today we are discussing the importance of praying for others. Prayer for others demonstrates we are not selfish and that we care about others. It demonstrates our obedience to God since He asks us to do so. And it gives us a feeling of joy and satisfaction when we do so.

In today's scripture lesson King Herod has just arranged to kill James, one of the disciples, because he knew it would please the Jews, who hated the Christians. This is the grandson of the King Herod during the time of Jesus. Seeing how his execution of James pleased the Jews, he decided to execute Peter also, the leader of the disciples. Meanwhile, at the home of Mary, one of the disciples, all the rest of the disciples were praying for Peter.

It was close to the time of Passover so Herod had him arrested and put in prison, guarded by 16 soldiers. But God was not ready for Peter to die. An angel was sent to Peter during the night while he was sleeping between two guards with chains on his hands and feet. The angel told Peter to get up, dress, put his cloak on, and leave. Immediately the chains fell away. Peter thought this was all a vision at the time. The guards heard and saw nothing. Peter followed the angel out of the cell and at the prison gate it swung open by itself and he went into the street. Then he realized this was the work of the Lord.

Peter walked to Mary's house and knocked at the gate. The maidservant recognized him but was so full of joy she did not open the gate but ran to tell the others. They did not believe her but when they heard him knocking they thought it was his angel. Then when Peter came in they realized it was really he and were amazed. Peter asked for silence and told the story. Everyone was astounded but they realized that God had done it all.

The power of prayer cannot be underestimated. If you pray for something and if it is a selfless prayer and sincere and within God's plan, it will be accomplished in His way and timeframe. Always remember these things when you pray. Always end your prayers with "but let your will be done Lord". This acknowledges that God will accomplish and answer your prayer in His way and His timeframe not yours. If you are praying without doing this, sometimes your prayers may not fit within God's plans and purposes so it may seem that your prayers go unanswered and it may frustrate you. But if you pray for God's will to be done then you can relax and find peace knowing that you have turned over your request to God and now He will address it in His own way. God is all knowing and all powerful so who better to answer your prayer the best way? Let's pray now for someone you know who needs God's help.

WHY DOES GOD WANT US TO PRAY AND HOW DOES HE HEAR ALL OUR PRAYERS?

Here are a few tough questions about prayer.

God knows everything so why do we need to pray?

- Our prayer demonstrates our faith that we believe in God and that He will answer our prayer.

- It acknowledges that we are powerless to control our lives.

- It demonstrates that we are humble and recognize God's power.

- It demonstrates our obedience.

Does God hear everyone's prayers or only Christians'?

He hears everyone's prayers but He answers them according to His will. Factors involve God's plans, our sincerity, what the prayer is, if it is unselfish, if it advances God's causes, if it helps someone toward salvation. Only God knows. But the prayers may not be answered if they are selfish, go against any of God's laws, and go against His plans.

Do all our prayers get answered?

The Bible says in Mark 11:24 that whatever we ask for in prayer, if we believe we have received it, it will be ours. So we can have anything we want? As I said, if they are unselfish, sincere, advance God's causes, help others somehow, help deepen your relationship with God, and if they fit His plans and timeframe.

How can God hear 2 billion prayers at the same time?

In our world we have only 3 space dimensions (height, width, length) and one time dimension (always moving forward). But God was outside the universe when He created it so He exists outside all time and space, and enters our time and space whenever He chooses. God exists in many more dimensions than we do. Since he is omnipresent (everywhere at the same time), He hears them all.

So even scientifically Einstein's theory of relativity states that at the instant the universe began there were perhaps 9 other dimensions or more. So the concept of God existing in multiple dimensions does not contradict science. If God has the ability to add just one more time dimension and also to be everywhere at the same time, He can hear all 2 billion prayers. God can break one instant in time into an infinite number of pieces and because He can exist in the present, past and future simultaneously, an instant for us can be an infinite amount of time for Him.

JULY LESSONS

STEPHEN PREACHED

Scripture verses	Acts 6:8 – 7:60
High level key topic	When you know what you believe, it gives you courage to endure

SCRIPTURAL LESSON NARRATIVE

Stephen was one of Jesus' disciples and preached the gospel faithfully. When he preached to a certain group of people in the synagogue, a great debate began. They did not agree with Stephen's preaching but could not dispute it. The crowd became angry, invested false statements about Stephen and dragged him in front of the Sanhedrin, the Jewish ruling council, saying that he blasphemed. All these things were lies. When the Sanhedrin asked him about his preaching, Stephen told the story of Israel and Moses and how everything had happened up to that point. At the end, he criticized them as not being true believers and said that Jesus was in heaven now, sitting at the right hand of God. That enraged everyone who felt that was blasphemy and they took him outside the city and stoned him to death. While this happened, Stephen looked up to God and asked Him to forgive them.

Could you endure such torture and still insist that the gospel was true? Cling to the truth of Christ and don't let anything stop you or make you uncomfortable about sharing the gospel. God will be with you always and see you through anything that happens to you. You have to believe and trust in Him.

HOW TO SHARE THE GOSPEL
AND EXPLAIN HOW WE KNOW IT IS TRUE

Today's memory verse, 1 Peter 3:15, is the foundation for Christian apologetics. This verse commands us to be prepared to explain how we know that our faith is true. Can you do that?

As you grow older and mature as a Christian, sharing the gospel will become a little easier but only if you try to share it. Otherwise it will never be easy and never feel comfortable.

In order to share the gospel at your age, you can take the simple route and tell your friends about how Jesus sacrificed Himself to give them an opportunity to live eternally with Him in heaven, and invite them to come to church with you to find out more.

But what can we say about Jesus and Christianity that we know is true because the evidence leads us there?

Here are a few things.

1. We know that God exists because He created the universe and all living things. Science has no evidence or reasonable explanation for how these miracles occurred. The complexity of life and design of the universe requires an unbelievably intelligent and all powerful Source. That is another way of describing God.

2. The Bible is true. It is a historical record with thousands of manuscript copies still available that date back to the generation of Jesus. It is written by eyewitnesses and reporters who interviewed eyewitnesses who saw Jesus' miracles, saw Him resurrected, and who performed miracles of their own. It is a true and accurate record of history.

3. The Bible tells us that Jesus is God and that the only way for eternal life in heaven is through Jesus.

4. So anyone who believes in Jesus and accepts Him as Lord is saved. Anyone who does not is not saved but doomed.

5. Because these things prove Christianity is true, then all other religions must be false because they all refuse to admit Jesus is God. Whatever is the opposite of true is false so all other religions are false.

Believe in Jesus and be confident sharing the gospel.

SAUL'S CONVERSION	
Scripture verses	Acts 8:1-3; 9:1-31
High level key topic	God's chosen will find Him

SCRIPTURAL LESSON NARRATIVE

Last week Stephen was stoned because he preached the gospel. That day, except for the apostles, many disciples scattered to other cities because a great persecution broke out against anyone who followed Jesus. The person who stood by and kept Stephen's robes while it happened was Saul. He was a member of the Sanhedrin and agreed with the persecution of Christians. He was so determined and vicious about stopping Christianity that he began going house to house and putting people in jail if they followed the Way (early name for Christianity due to John 14:6).

Next, his vicious attitude led him to request letters from the Jewish leaders to chase after those who scattered from Jerusalem and went to Damascus. Letters were sent to the Damascus synagogues instructing the leaders there to identify anyone with the Way and hold them captive for Paul to retrieve them to Jerusalem to be put in jail and prosecuted.

But while travelling to Damascus to pick up the prisoners, a great light flashed and Saul and his followers were stopped in their tracks. Jesus appeared to him and said, "Saul, why do you persecute me?" Saul said, "Who are you Lord?" and the reply was, "I am Jesus". Saul's friends did not hear the voice. Jesus blinded him and told him to go to Damascus to find Ananias who would heal him and that Saul would then preach the gospel in Jesus' name. At the same time, Ananias was given a vision saying that he should seek out a man named Saul, heal him and baptize him. Ananias knew who Saul was and was afraid because of what Saul had done to disciples.

When Ananias found him, he healed him, restored his sight, baptized him and told him to go preach the gospel. Immediately Saul went to the synagogues to tell everyone what happened and to persuade them that Jesus is the Son of God. They could not counter his arguments and proof but sought to kill him. He was helped out of the city to escape and went back to Jerusalem to visit with the apostles. They were nervous about seeing him but Barnabas explained everything that happened and that he would become known as Paul and preach the gospel to the gentiles.

When Jesus calls you to share the gospel in his name, will you find a way to have the courage and do it?

HOW DOES SALVATION ACTUALLY OCCUR?

We have free will. But God knew before time began who would be saved. His omniscience allows him to see the future and know when someone will be saved. God wills salvation to be available to all but not all will accept. Many eminent modern theologians believe that through general revelation (nature) we are able to recognize there is a Creator. When that happens we become seekers and God continually presents opportunities for us to learn more about Him and eventually be introduced to the gospel and have an opportunity for salvation.

Part of the role of the Holy Spirit is to constantly urge people to choose salvation. At the moment that the Holy Spirit recognizes in your heart that you believe and accept Jesus as Lord, He convicts you, changes you forever, and takes on a more active role to influence your life. You can call on the Holy Spirit for help through prayer.

NEW JERUSALEM – HEAVEN ON EARTH

Scripture verses	New Jerusalem description - Revelation 4:3-6, 5:9-14, 7:9-12, 11:15-17, 21: 11-17, 22:5, Ezek. 1:13-14, 10:6-9 Rewards in heaven - Psalm 58:11; Luke 18:29-30; Colossians 3:23-24
High level key topic	New Jerusalem will be heaven on earth. When we are in Christ, we have paradise to look forward to one day

SCRIPTURAL LESSON NARRATIVE

When Jesus returns, He will save Israel at the battle of Armageddon, vanquish all evil and chain Satan for a thousand years while Jesus rules on earth with the help of all Christians who are brought down from heaven with Him. Then after unchaining Satan for a short period of time while being allowed to see if any believers can be tempted, Satan and all who follow him are banished to the Lake of Fire forever. Then the entire world is transformed and New Jerusalem is created as heaven on earth.

What will it be like? Let's explore and see if you can follow the description and draw an amazing picture of what it will be like.

- we will be in a state of constant anticipation of excitement, like before a big football game

- we will have special bodies that do not wear out

- we will not experience any pain, suffering, regret, sorry, tears, sadness, or any bad experiences

Description of New Jerusalem

- it will be a cube, 1500 miles wide, tall, and long, would cover 65% of continental US – Rev. 21:11-17 describes the dimensions, gates and wall

    o Jesus went to prepare a mansion for each of us

    o with 2.2 billion Christians, each person currently would have about 3500 acres perfectly suited to our ideal vision of our likes and interests o there is no natural light but it is always light there, from the direct radiance of God. there is no darkness - Revel 22:5

o a great wall, probably made of jasper(diamond), is about 250 ft. tall and surrounds the circumference of the cube

o the wall is supported by 12 layers of precious stones - sapphire, emerald, topaz, amethyst and others

o the 12 gates are carved out of giant pearls (pearly gates)

o the gates will never close

o 12 boulevards go from each gate to the mountaintop and are divided roads, with a portion of the great river running thru each, coming from the throne at the top of the mountain

o a great throne is at the top of the mount for Father God and one to the right for Jesus

o countless numbers of heavenly beings surround Them (cherubim – Ezek. 1:13-14; 10:6-9) and 4 seraphim hover above the thrones (angelic beings with 3 sets of wings- one set covers their face, one their feet, and the other is to fly)

o the beings all sing and chant – Rev. 5:11-12; Rev. 5:9-10; Rev. 7:9-12; Rev. 11:15-17

o there is a rainbow around the throne, emerald in color - Rev 4:3-6

o there is a large crystal platform beneath the throne - Rev 4:6

o the 12 roads are made of pure gold, as is the city itself

o on both sides of the river is the Tree of Life, with 12 different fruit, each produced one per month

o but there is no time in New Jerusalem. It lasts forever.

o as the leaves fall from the tree, they enrich the soil

o just inside each of the 12 gates the terrain slopes upward at a 63 degree angle culminating in the top of the Mount of the Lord where God's throne will be o 270 times higher than Mt. Everest at the peak

o top would be about where Denver is if the west gate started at the California beach - what a view from our mansion right?

Other notes:

- we will have rewards in heaven - Psalm 58:11; Luke 18:29-30; Colossians 3:23-24

- we will eat from the Tree of Life

- we will receive a new name known only to God

- we will be clothed in white garments

- we will each receive a crown of righteousness, a crown of glory and a crown of life

- we will have a higher place of order than the angels and we will judge the angels

- each moment we will be filled with wonder and awe and amazement, never boredom

- we will experience God's presence and know Him

- all anyone needs do to experience this unbelievable joy forever, is to say and mean from the heart a simple prayer, something like:

  o Jesus come into my life, forgive my sins, and be my Lord

  o then they will hear and witness the following in New Jerusalem – Rev. 5:11-14

BE THANKFUL	
Scripture verses	Luke 17:11-19
High level key topic	God wants us to thank others and be thankful for them

SCRIPTURAL LESSON NARRATIVE

We live in a world and particularly in our country where we have most everything we want. This causes us to easily forget where all our blessings come from. We expect to have what we need. We expect to be taken care of. We expect to have food to eat and enough money to do most of what we want. We have so much that we take it for granted. When everything goes so easily in our lives, false pride steps in and influences us to think we made it all happen and sometimes that we have no need for God.

Today's lesson is to remind us to be thankful for everything we have. It is easy to be thankful when someone does something nice for you and you have been taught to say thank you. But can you also thank God even during times of trouble or when something awful strikes you or your family? Too often people easily accept when things go right and then blame God when something bad happens. How could you allow this God?

But God wants us to be thankful in all cases. Can you find it in yourself to be thankful during a tragedy? Maybe you would say there is nothing to be thankful for. But you don't know God's mind and His plans. Could it be that a tragedy would bring you closer to God and influence you to depend more on Him for support and guidance? Could something good come out of a tragedy? Could it be that you are so rebellious that only a tragedy wakes you up to your need for God? Could a tragedy cause someone to become a seeker and even believer? Could a tragedy make you realize you can't control your life? Could a tragedy make you begin to wonder more about God and cause you to search the Bible for more understanding? Yes to all. We can't fully know God's mind. But we can trust Him in all circumstances, even the desperate and bad ones. A thankful heart opens us to messages God may want to communicate. While you give thanks it is virtually impossible to sin or curse God. So the more time you invest in thanks to God, the more God will provide understanding and support to you and the less often you will sin.

In today's lesson, Jesus is confronted by 10 lepers. Leprosy was a horrible disease in old times, with open sores and loss of feelings in nerves. Lepers were considered unclean and were not allowed within the gates of the city because the disease was highly contagious. In this story, Jesus told the lepers they were healed and sent them to talk to the priest who would then declare them clean again so they could approach the city and even worship together again. As the lepers were on their way, they became healed. But one leper returned to Jesus and thanked Him for healing him. Jesus declared that the man's faith had healed him and asked aloud why the other lepers had not returned also to thank him. The story shows us the example of people who may turn to God for help and then forget to thank Him even once He answers our prayers. Be thankful in all circumstances and you will stay closer to God.

WHAT DO ATHEISTS THINK ABOUT CHRISTIANS?

Please spend some time reviewing the following web site – www.christianitydis-proved.com. Or google for other atheist web sites for this review.

This web site is written by and supported by atheists. An atheist is someone who believes there is no God. Often times, they make vicious attacks on Christians and try their best to declare us fools and that faith has no reason and Christianity is not true. That is what this web site is all about.

As you get older you must prepare yourself to understand that many people do not think like Christians and many people you will encounter in life feel very negatively towards Christians. By reviewing this web site you will see some of their arguments. You may be surprised and perhaps confused as you read them. You will encounter negative ideas you may have never heard before.

Sadly, there is even a section for testimonials of supposed ex-Christians who have now become atheists and they tell their stories and list their reasons. In most cases it is either due to misinformation and misunderstanding or willful rebellion from God.

Christian apologetics is the study of evidence that defends the truth of Christianity from such attacks as mentioned on the web site. Be fully aware that many people have good questions and concerns about Christianity. But also become aware that there are good answers to these questions. Unfortunately, most Christians do not know the answers and do not know how to respond to these challenges.

If you think it is important to be able to respond and know the answers to these issues, then maybe you will begin your own search for the truth. Jesus said the truth will set you free.

Never be afraid when you hear a surprising or very good argument against Christianity. Jesus is the truth, the Bible is true, and there is nothing that will ever be able to validly contradict the Bible. If you read or hear something that concerns you, seek the answers but don't lose your faith or fear that something has been discovered that will shake your faith in Christianity.

AUGUST LESSONS (END OF YEAR)

As mentioned, August is a mix of the last teaching for the previous class and the first teaching for the new class. So these are the last lessons for the class for the year before the new class arrives. Typically, we use them over and over each year.

REVELATION	
Scripture verses	Revelation
High level key topic	God revealed to us what His final plans are for humanity. Be prepared for Jesus' second coming and share the gospel with everyone

SCRIPTURAL LESSON NARRATIVE

We live in increasingly difficult and dangerous times. We know Jesus promised to return one day. Will we be ready?

Consider these things predicted to be signs of the end of times by Jesus in Mathew 24, Daniel 9:24, Revelation, Isaiah, and elsewhere:

- Major environmental changes

    o Increase in major earthquakes (Matthew)

    o Increased radiation (Revelation)

    o Significant shifts in weather/temperature patterns (Mark, Revelation)

    o Famine/pestilence (Revelation)

- Technology

    o Explosion in knowledge increase (Daniel)

    o Gospel will be taught worldwide, then the end (Matthew)

    o Destructive weapons, no flesh will be saved (Matthew, Zechariah)

- Major decline in moral values

- o #1 cause of death is murder if you include abortion

- o Increase in false religions – Islam, Hinduism, New Age, occult

- o Compromised truth – relativism

- • Global unity

  - o Heading toward one world religion – Chrislam? (Revelation)

  - o Proposals to evolve to global currency (Revelation)

  - o Constant suggestions from Europe and elsewhere for a one world political system (Revelation)

  - o Whole world against Israel – today's reality (Revelation)

  - o Even the US trying to force Israel to give most of Jerusalem away – against the Bible

    - > Pursued and suggested by the Obama administration over and over

  - o Jerusalem will be a burden to all (Ezekiel)

  - o Israel will fill the world with fruit - #3 exporter of fruit, sells flowers to Holland, from desert to vegetation

  - o Temple must be rebuilt – preparations ongoing (Revelation)

- • Other

  - o Wars and rumors of great wars

  - o Increase in volcanic activity

  - o Persecution of Christians

  - o Great lawlessness

  - o Little love for others

The question is whether we are in the end of times period even now? Every generation thinks so but the evidence mounts. The Bible tells us we must be prepared because no one knows when the thief may rob your house. But if you knew it was going to happen, you would be ready. Are you satisfied you have accepted Christ and done everything to talk with your family and friends and others about Jesus? Is there anyone you are concerned about? Don't wait.

WHAT HAPPENS DURING THE 7 YEAR TRIBULATION PERIOD?

There is much debate and differences of opinion about the rapture and second coming. Rapture means a time when all believers are brought up into heaven. Some think it happens just before the tribulation period, some after, some think it is the same as the second coming, and other opinions vary.

21 JUDGMENTS DURING TRIBULATION

7 Seals

1. Revelation 6:1-2 – white horse, antichrist, peace treaty

2. Revelation 6:3-4 – red horse, Russia, war

3. Revelation 6:-5-6 – black horse, famine, economic disaster

4. Revelation 6:7-8 – pale horse, ⊠ die, starvation, disease

5. Revelation 6:9-11 – Christians saved and killed

6. Revelation 6:12-17 – great earthquake, 114,000 Jews saved & millions of gentiles

7. Revelation 8:1-2 – Contains 7 trumpet judgments

7 Trumpets

1. Revelation 8:6-7 – hail and fire, 1/ of earth burned up

2. Revelation 8:8-9 – Giant meteor into sea – 1/3 of sea turns to blood, 1/ living creatures die

3. Revelation 8:10-11 – meteor, 1/3 of rivers and wells poisoned

4. Revelation 8:12 – 1/3 light of sun, moon, stars extinguished

5. Revelation 9:1-11 – Satan unleashes demons from pit to torture but not kill

6. Revelation 9:12-19 – 4 wicked angels loosed, 1/3 die

7. Revelation 11:15-19 – 2nd coming of Christ

7 bowls (simultaneous)

1. Revelation 16:2 – people covered with sores, plague

2. Revelation 16:3 – Sea turns to blood

3. Revelation 16:4 – other waters turn to blood

4. Revelation 16:8-9 – people scorched with great heat

5. Revelation 16:10-11 – darkness over the world

6. Revelation 16:12 – world war

7. Revelation 16:17-21 – mighty earthquake, Armageddon

Other

- Revelation 19:20 – antichrist/false prophet thrown into Lake of Fire

- Revelation 20:4-6 – Jesus reigns on earth for 1000 yrs. and we help rule

- Revelation 20: 7-10 – Satan released for a while then thrown back into Lake of fire

- Revelation 20:12-13 – Dead are judged

- Revelation 21:1-6 – New heaven on earth (New Jerusalem)

    o No seas, no pain, no light needed

THE ASSIGNMENT

Scripture verses	Acts 14
High level key topic	God wants us to tell everyone about Jesus

SCRIPTURAL LESSON NARRATIVE

Congratulations rising sixth graders! I'm so blessed to have known each of you. It has been a privilege and honor to know you and share with you many key messages about God, Jesus, the Bible, Christianity and how and why Christianity is not only unique, but is grounded in truth.

As we finish your year today, the lesson is a fitting one. Once we become followers of Christ, it is God's command that we not only believe, but also practice the responsibilities and commands He has given us of being a Christian. The final part of that journey is to spread the good news of Jesus to others. Can you believe in God so much that you try hard every day to be more like Jesus and to be prepared to share that good news with others as you encounter them in your life? It's not easy being a Christian. You will endure persecution as Jesus did. You are called upon to live a good life and help others and be role models for others. You will have to deal with ridicule and skepticism and even hatred. Will that stop you from being a Christian? Will that stop you from telling others about Jesus? Or will that motivate you to the critical need to tell even more people about Christ?

Each of you has a unique set of gifts from God and has a unique calling. Pray constantly for God to lead you in your steps and ways. Then enjoy each day that God has made and rejoice in it. He will lead your steps and you will find your calling if you stay constantly connected to Him.

HOW DO I USE MY APOLOGETICS KNOWLEDGE GOING FORWARD?

You have learned a great deal about the evidence available that points to the reasonable conclusion that Christianity is in fact true. You have learned about the scientific evidence that points to God's existence and Creator of all things. You have learned about the philosophical evidence that shows that all religions cannot be true because they teach opposites. If Christianity is true, then no other religion is true because they teach that Jesus is not God. You have learned about the historical evidence that points to the reliability of the New Testament. Christianity is the only religion that has scriptures based on historical evidence and eyewitness claims.

What do you do with this awareness and knowledge? First, use it to maintain your own faith during difficult times. Do not let anyone convince you that God does not exist or that the Bible is not true. When you have doubts; pray harder and more often. Perhaps do your own study of the evidence that points to the truth of Christianity. When you have difficult problems and pain and suffering in your life, don't blame God or doubt God. He has a plan to make everything that happens work for the good of those who love Him. Instead, thank Him for all your blessings. Thank Him for giving you the opportunity to prove your faith through difficult times.

When you encounter others who make false claims about Christianity be assured that you have the truth. Be bold yet gentle and respectful and let them know that Christianity is founded on truth and evidence that logically points to Christianity and God as the answers to life's most important questions. All that is needed is to keep an open mind and to study the real evidence without bias.

As you progress to college and meet more people who are not believers, remember the lessons you have learned. Do not let new friends and even professors who you admire convince you of anything against God, Jesus and the Bible that I have taught you. If something comes up that causes you worry, pray and seek God's word. Or contact me. Even if you cannot find the answer immediately, be assured that God's truth in scripture and God's truth in nature will never contradict. Somewhere and sometime there will be an answer that will lead to the recognition of God as the Maker of all things and Jesus as His Son.

Rejoice and remember!

EXTRA LESSONS

JESUS GIVES HOPE	
Scripture verses	Matthew 8:1-13
High level key topic	Jesus wants us to know and love Him. Jesus did miracles to prove His love, prove His deity, and give us hope for the future

SCRIPTURAL LESSON NARRATIVE

Jesus gives hope. What does that mean? What is hope? The dictionary defines hope in two ways: to desire with an expectation of attainment; and trust. It seems this definition perfectly fits what Jesus means to Christians. By doing miracles, helping others, being humble, showing he cared, living a sinless life and sacrificing all to prove His love for us He causes us to truly believe in Him, in His message, and in our future with Him. Who Jesus actually was proves that we can trust His words. He stated that if we believe in Him and follow Him we can have eternal life with Him. That is our hope and we have every reason to believe we can trust Him and attain eternal life as He stated.

In Jesus' time medicine was virtually non-existent. One of the ways Jesus helped others believe in Him was by doing miracles, particularly healing sick and crippled people who were everywhere. Society in those days shunned these people and believed they were that way because of sin. Jesus spent most of His time healing sick people and shattered the idea that it was due to sin.

Our story today involves two healing miracles. First, He encountered a man with leprosy. Leprosy was a terrible skin disease, highly contagious, and those who had it were often forced out of the city into caves to form their own communities away from the rest of the people. The leper came up to Him and said he knew Jesus could heal him if he was willing. Jesus agreed, touched him, and the man was immediately healed. Jesus asked him to go to the priest and be cleansed spiritually but to tell no one what had happened. Why? (sometimes the people in a particular area would not become believers so Jesus did not intend the message for them. Other times it might be because Jesus was not ready for those people to know about Him yet).

Then a Roman centurion came up to Him and explained that His servant was ill and dying. Jesus said He would come and heal him. But the centurion said He was not worthy for Jesus to come into His home but that with just His authority to command such as the centurion did, speaking it so would make it happen. Jesus said He had not seen such faith in all of Israel. He spoke for the servant to be healed and it was done immediately.

Both these events are examples of extreme faith. They truly believed who Jesus was and what He could do. That is why Jesus was so impressed with them and willing to immediately do what they asked. This is also a lesson for us. If we can have such faith, our prayers can also be answered. Believe in Jesus, ask Him for whatever you need and He will provide it in His own way. It may not always be exactly as you expect but trust Him. In Jesus we have hope for the present and the future with Him.

DID JESUS REALLY DIE AND RISE FROM THE DEAD?

Many deny that Jesus was resurrected, others deny He died and those of other religions and nonbelievers all deny He was God. Paul said that if Christ did not die and was raised that we are all still dead in our sins. Essentially, Christianity is false if Jesus did not die and was raised from the dead. So this is a critical issue for Christians and everyone. What is the evidence to support that Jesus actually died and was resurrected?

Let's examine this purely as though the NT documents are merely historical and not inspired. In other words leave God out of the picture for now and just look at the historical facts from the earliest Greek documents that describe the events. These documents were written within a couple decades of Jesus' death. Keep in mind that virtually all historical scholars generally believe the stories of Alexander the Great yet the earliest documents about his life were written 400 years later. In fact, the vast majority of bible scholars and critics agree with these facts below:

JESUS WAS RESURRECTED

1. *Jesus was buried in a tomb by a Jewish leader of the Sanhedrin, Joseph of Arimathea.* So the burial and grave and location was known to everyone, Christian, Jewish and Roman. There is no other competing burial story about Jesus.

2. *The tomb was found empty by women*. Numerous independent sources. The body was never found. The Romans wanted to find the body to prove He had not been resurrected. Jewish tradition immediately claimed the body was stolen by the disciples. But that assumes the tomb was empty.

3. *12 Appearances of the resurrected Jesus*. He was witnessed by most of the apostles, a crowd of over 500 and then by Paul 3 years later. No one ever came forward to deny the sightings and many were still alive when the scriptures were recorded. 1 Corinthians 15:3-8 quotes an early creed that goes back to within months of Jesus' death and resurrection.

4. *The remarkable change of behavior by disciples*. Before the resurrected Jesus appeared, the disciples were timid and fearful men. They ran when Jesus was arrested. Only John was present at the crucifixion. Jesus' brother James was not a follower until He saw the resurrected Jesus. Peter, the leader of the disciples, denied Jesus three times. They were weak and afraid. But after the appearances by the resurrected Jesus they be-

came bold and unafraid. They preached the gospel so aggressively that all but John were executed. Why would they give up their lives if they didn't believe it? Why would Christianity expand so rapidly if it did not happen?

As stated, virtually all scholars, even critical scholars, agree with the above facts. The only disagreement is the conclusion and what the facts mean. Most just say they don't know. But some other unpersuasive arguments have been put forth. No naturalistic explanation has been accepted by any majority of scholars.

OBJECTIONS TO THE RESURRECTION

1. *Jesus only appeared to die.* A frequent Muslim claim. But there were dozens of eyewitnesses at the crucifixion. The Roman guards were expert executioners and knew when someone was dead. If they were mistaken they would forfeit their own lives and be executed for their failure. How could He survive all His wounds for three days with no medical care and three days in a damp, empty tomb? Even medical experts today who read the description of the crucifixion and circumstances have declared that there is no doubt He would have died.

2. *The body was stolen.* This is the Jewish view. But how could a few timid and weak disciples overpower numerous Roman guards, find a way to open a sealed tomb with a huge stone in front, and get away with it and no one ever found out or found the body of Jesus?

3. *The women went to the wrong tomb.* Everyone knew where the tomb was. Joseph of Arimathea was a disciple himself and told everyone where it was.

4. *It was not Jesus but someone else.* Another Muslim claim. But everyone knew what Jesus looked like. Would the Roman soldiers risk their lives to bury the wrong man?

5. *Everyone hallucinated.* But we know from modern science and psychiatry that mass hallucinations do not occur.

6. *New Testament was a lie.* But as stated, these are historical documents accepted by the vast majority of historical and bible scholars; even the most critical of those including Bart Ehrman.

7. *Miracles are not possible.* This is the conclusion of those who believe in naturalism and materialism and the claims of many scientists and atheists. But when they define science as the search for natural causes they violate a law of logic. All causes are either natural or unnatural (supernatural). They have no way of knowing if some causes could be supernatu-

ral. Clearly, the creation of the universe and creation of first life have no satisfactory explanations from science and the best explanation points to God's existence. And if you read Keener's book called *Miracles*, thousands of them have been recorded in modern history and in ancient history. So miracles are possible.

So we have to ask ourselves, what is the best explanation of the facts? What do you think? God raised Jesus from the dead is the best explanation of the facts.

Be confident that the miracle of the resurrection occurred. Not only did it occur but it was planned. And it was planned to provide salvation for you and everyone if we only believe and follow Jesus. Jesus died for our sins and was resurrected, and His spirit lives within us when we accept Him as Savior. Glorify His name and follow Him and His teachings.

ALIVE FOREVER!

Scripture verses	Matthew 26:36-28:10
High level key topic	Jesus died and was resurrected to save us from our sins. With that knowledge, we should tell others about Him.

SCRIPTURAL LESSON NARRATIVE

Easter is perhaps the greatest day for Christians. We celebrate the day Jesus conquered death and rose from the grave to save us from our sins. Why did Jesus have to die? Because we all have sinned, God is all-holy and just and cannot tolerate sin. The penalty for sin is death. But God loved us so much He created a way to secure eternal life for us because we could do nothing to save ourselves. God took the form of a man, allowed Himself to be ridiculed, tortured and killed. The blood of Christ was used to bear the price of our sins and wash them away in God's eyes forever. Then Jesus rose from the dead to fulfill prophecy and to be at Father God's right hand again. The precious gift of our salvation is offered to us for free. That is what we call grace; a free gift that we don't deserve. All we need do is accept Christ in our hearts as our Savior and Lord and follow His teachings. Will you pray and acknowledge your acceptance of our Lord Jesus if you have not already?

The story of Jesus' resurrection starts that night of the Last Supper. Later Jesus led the disciples to the Garden of Gethsemane to pray. Three times Jesus went to pray and asked the disciples to stand guard. Three times Jesus prayed for God to find another way out for Jesus but finally that God's will be done. Three times Jesus found the disciples asleep. Then Judas came and kissed Jesus and betrayed Him to the guards to be arrested. Peter cut off the ear of one soldier in rebellion but Jesus healed the man and told Peter that those who yield the sword will die by the sword. The guards took Jesus, beat him and spit upon Him, and all the disciples ran away.

Peter followed at a distance as the guards took Jesus in the middle of the night to the high priest, Caiaphas, and into his courtyard. After grilling Him with questions and presenting false witnesses, Caiaphas finally demanded that Jesus admit if He was the Messiah and Son of God. Jesus acknowledged it. Then Caiaphas declared this was blasphemy and called for Jesus to be executed.

Early in the morning daylight Jesus was taken to the Roman Governor Pilate's court and they demanded Pilate declare Him guilty and crucify Him. Pilate questioned Jesus but Jesus was silent. Pilate finally asked if He was God's Son and Jesus admitted it. But Pilate found no wrong-doing and washed His hands of Jesus' blood in front of everyone. The crowd yelled for Jesus to be crucified. Pilate had offered to release one man as a gift because it was Passover time but the crowd chose Barabbas, a thief and murderer. Pilate had Jesus scourged (flogged, whipped). The guards then made a crown of thorns and spit on Him and beat him. They made a cross and forced Jesus to carry it on the way to be crucified at Calvary. Simon the Cyrene volunteered to carry the cross the rest of the way when Jesus was too weak. They nailed Jesus to the cross at nine in the morning. From noon to 3 PM the sky went dark. Then Jesus gave up His spirit in His last breath and died. There was an earthquake and the curtain in the temple was split in two and the tombs of some were opened and they became alive and walked around town to be seen by many.

A follower of Jesus, Joseph of Arimathea, and member of the Jewish body of leaders, paid for a tomb and took the body of Jesus, anointed Him, and wrapped Him in bandages and buried Him in a tomb and rolled a large stone in front. The next day the Jewish leaders pleaded with Pilate to place a guard at the tomb for fear that the body would be stolen according to the prophecies of His resurrection. The tomb was sealed and a guard was placed there.

The following day the women went to the tomb but when they arrived there was an earthquake and the stone came open and an angel appeared saying that Jesus was gone and resurrected as He had promised. As they left the tomb Jesus appeared to them and greeted them. They bowed and kissed His feet. He asked them to go and tell the others what had happened and to meet Him in Galilee.

Our Lord had risen!

COMPARISON OF WORLDVIEWS

Now let's take a look at the three main worldviews. A worldview is how one sees reality. Your view of how the world and reality are.

WORLDVIEWS (HOW YOU SEE REALITY)

GREEK - THEOS=GOD, A=AGAINST, PAN=ALL

	ATHEISM (against theism)	THEISM (belief in God)	PANTHEISM (belief in many/all gods)
What it means	There is no God	God created all	god is all/god is nature/everything is part of god
Which religions		Christianity, Judaism, Islam	Hinduism, Buddhism, New Age
Evidence for	• Based on naturalism/materialism • (natural world is all there is)	• Creation of universe • Creation of life • Fine tuning of universe • Moral argument	Old scriptures/legends
Evidence against	• Naturalism is irrational • No grounds for morals • Denies evidence for theism	• The heart • Illogical assumptions • Erroneous science arguments • Judaism denies NT/Jesus • Islam denies NT/Jesus • Islam has terrible historical evidence	• No eyewitnesses • No historical basis
Fits best view of reality		Only Christianity	

LOVING MY FAMILY

Scripture verses	Gen. 46-50
High level key topic	God wants family members to take care of each other

SCRIPTURAL LESSON NARRATIVE

God told Jacob to move his 70+ member family to Egypt. This was after the grueling story of Joseph and his miraculous escape from his brothers' evil and rise to power as second in command to Pharaoh in Egypt. During the 7 prophesied good years Joseph stored grain for the 7 years of famine. Pharaoh granted a large parcel of land to Jacob and his family. After all the evil his brothers tried to create for him Joseph forgave them all and wept with joy as they were reunited.

There is a great lesson here for all of us. Often times family members have squabbles and disagreements. But they are our blood and we should always forgive them no matter what because God forgives us no matter what. When we become a mature Christian we also realize this attitude of forgiveness and love should extend to everyone; not just family. If Joseph could forgive his brothers for what they did to him and still find love in their hearts and if God can forgive us for how we sin against Him and others then we can be big enough to forgive others also.

IS THE NEW TESTAMENT TEXT RELIABLE?

Most Christians do not realize why many Bible critics and non-Christians say that the Bible cannot be trusted as reliable. Children in Sunday school are not typically taught why there are issues at all. We are taught that the Bible is the Word of God, that it is inerrant (without errors) and should believe it. We are taught it is a historical record and has been tested through time. All of this is true so what are the issues of criticism? Much of this information may initially surprise you but you can be confident it has been resolved and that you can trust that the Bible is in fact reliable.

1. The Bible is a collection of scriptures from many authors over many decades and even centuries. The Bible as you see it was not written in a continuous way like the novels you read. The NT alone has nine different authors. So all the scriptures and even ancient scriptures from the OT were collected about AD 325 at a council of elders. There they decided what would be included or not included in one continuous book, which we now call the Bible. Some disagree with the methods they used to determine what went into the book and was God's Word. There are other scriptures that people refer to like the Gospel of Thomas, or Gospel of Judas, that were not included. But their method was valid: they chose based on scriptures written by apostles or prophets and those that were commonly accepted in the early days as authoritative.

2. There is not an original Bible or original document of any of the books in the Bible. This may surprise you but everything we have is a copy of copies called manuscripts. So we as Christians believe the Bible is the inerrant Word of God but when we say that we are talking about the originals. The ones left now do have errors. Over the years all the originals were lost and only the copies made by scribes for distribution are left. But we have more copies of manuscripts from the bible than any other ancient text. We have 5700 NT Greek manuscripts in whole or part and over 10,000 in other languages.

3. The earliest manuscript piece dates back to 90 -115 AD. This is called the John Ryland fragment and was written on papyrus. This is from a reed and spread out like a parchment. It contains just a few verses from the book of John. We have about a dozen manuscripts from the second century but all are fragments. It does include 3 of the 4 Gospels and 9 of Paul's

letters. We have 64 manuscripts from the third century and 48 from the fourth. So we have 124 manuscripts within 300 years of the originals. The two most accurate are called P75 and Codex Vaticanus B. These go back to early second century. P75 has large portions of Luke and John. Codex B has most of the NT. The key is that comparing all the manuscript pieces against each other we find we have a high degree of accuracy and completeness and when we put them all together we have essentially the NT.

4. The manuscripts contain thousands of so-called errors. It is true that the manuscripts have many variations within. But most are due to copying errors, transcription errors, and changes of one letter or a word. But even with all the differences we do not have anything that affects any important Christian principle, meaning, doctrine or belief.

5. We have so many different versions of the Bible. Over the years, the Bible was translated into many different languages from the original Greek (NT), Hebrew and Aramaic (OT). This requires interpretation of what the words meant. This can be very tricky and scholars do not always agree. Over the centuries new versions were published as new groups of scholars changed some of the words to more common words used at the time, hence the King James version for example. But again, there are no important differences from all the original manuscripts.

6. Some scripture verses are added or left out in some of the manuscripts. For example, the story of the woman caught in adultery and Jesus proclaiming that whoever has no sin should cast the first stone (John 7:53-8:11). This story is not in the earliest manuscripts and we believe now was added later. There are at least several others as well. But most Bibles will have a note in brackets or in a footnote regarding these. Everything is disclosed for review and comparison. Another noteworthy one is the ending of Mark. Most scholars agree that it originally ended without the women telling anyone about the empty tomb. But we can know they did tell the disciples from the other gospels. The very fact that we know all these concerns and disclose them is a proof for the integrity of scripture. No one is hiding anything and these discrepancies or differences are easily explained and have no valid criticism to the authenticity and reliability of the Bible.

These are just a few of the criticisms. But worry not. The majority have been addressed satisfactorily enough to know with high probability that the scriptures are accurate and can be trusted. We do have the Word of God in its essence although some minor variations are accepted to have occurred.

JESUS CALLED DISCIPLES	
Scripture verses	Matthew 4:18-22, 9:9-13, Mark 1:16-20, 2:13-17, 3:13-19
High level key topic	Jesus also called us to follow Him and share the gospel

SCRIPTURAL LESSON NARRATIVE

After Jesus was baptized by John the Baptist, He began his ministry. First, he went around and called disciples. He found Peter and his brother Andrew fishing. Jesus told them He would make them fishers of men and asked them to follow Him and they did. Then He called James and John who were also brothers. Then Philip and Bartholomew. Matthew was a tax collector. Jesus ate at his house and Matthew followed him. Then Thomas and James, Thaddeus, Simon, and finally Judas.

The disciples did not hesitate when Jesus called them because they knew He was someone who had a great message for them and would teach them the ways to the kingdom of God. When Jesus calls you, will you follow and obey? Do you remember the ABCs of being a Christian?

WHAT DOES IT TAKE TO BE SAVED?

Ironically, there is not a single passage in the Bible that tells us everything we need to be saved. Some say that there are passages that indicate how to be saved such as "anyone who calls on the name of the Lord will be saved." And John 3:16. But neither of those verses mentions anything about admission of sin and turning away from your sin, asking for forgiveness, accepting God's grace and declaring that God is your savior.

Clearly it is not enough to merely believe that Jesus was God. Otherwise Satan and his demons are saved because they knew Jesus was God. So there must be more.

Calling out the Lord's name is not enough because true salvation comes from the heart not the lips.

So, Christians over time have put together the pieces of what is required for salvation. In Sunday school we teach these as the ABCs of becoming a Christian.

A – Admit you are a sinner and turn away from your sin

B – Believe that Jesus is God's Son and accept His gift of forgiveness for our sins

C- Confess that Jesus is your Savior and Lord

 Have all of you said a prayer about those at some point and sincerely meant it? If you have you will be saved and nothing can prevent you from being with Jesus forever. If you haven't will you do it today if you feel the Holy Spirit is urging you?

DON'T WORRY

Scripture verses	Matthew 6:25-34
High level key topic	When you focus on God, you don't have to worry

SCRIPTURAL LESSON NARRATIVE

Today's lesson is one of the hardest for us to manage and follow. It is about worrying. What things do you worry about?

It is natural for us to worry because we fear something bad might happen. But worry actually shows a lack of faith in God so we must be careful about it. Instead of worrying ourselves we should communicate with God and pray to turn over our worry to Him. Worry usually stems from wanting to be able to control our situation and make things turn out the way we want. But many things, even most things, are out of our control. When we put our time into worry it creates stress and makes it harder for us to function and may make things worse. And if it is something you cannot control anyway, why worry?

Instead, pray to God. This serves two purposes: first it shows you have faith in Him to take care of the situation or at least to help you get through it; second, it gives you peace of mind so you won't stress about it.

Our scripture today says that if God takes care of the birds and flowers but loves us even more, why should we think He won't take care of us? But there is a key to this whole scripture that we must understand. Who knows what it is? As is often the case, there is a conditional: it says "...seek first the kingdom of God and His righteousness, and these things will be provided for you." This means that if we ignore God and don't make Him primary in our lives, it creates separation from Him and that's when more bad things can happen. Because of sin in the world, without God, we are very weak and vulnerable to attacks by Satan and others who may do bad things. But with God as our focus, He will take care of us and help us through every situation. That is not to say nothing bad will ever happen to you. We've discussed how evil works and free will and natural events that we cannot control. But God will be there with you to help you through everything that happens in your life.

IS CHRISTIANITY THE BEST WORLDVIEW?

A worldview is much like what it sounds: your view of the world. In other words, your set of beliefs about the world and how things work that best explain the reality we live in.

There are 3 main worldviews: theism, atheism and agnosticism (some theologians might say pantheism and this is an acceptable alternative explanation/category)

Theism is a belief in God. Atheism is the belief there is no God. Agnosticism is the belief that you cannot know if there is a God. All religions and sets of beliefs fall under one of these.

In order to determine which worldview best describes reality it must explain four key questions:

1. Where do we come from
2. What is our purpose
3. How do we determine what is right and wrong
4. What is our final destiny

Let's take a look at each of the worldviews in regard to these questions:

QUESTION	THEISM	ATHEISM	AGNOSTICISM
Where do we come from?	God created us	Darwinian evolution but insufficient proof	Not sure
What is our purpose?	Learn about God Glorify His name Serve Him Serve others	No purpose, we operate based on blind chemical reactions in our brain	Not sure
How do we decide right and wrong?	God's Word God is the perfect standard of goodness	Each individual decides other than gov't laws	Not sure
What is our final destiny?	Heaven or hell	None	Not sure
The problem	Must accept Christ as Savior	Life has no meaning Leads to depression	No certainty in life about anything

So, you can see that belief in God, theism, has the best answers to life's most important and challenging questions.

HONESTY KEEPS US CLOSE TO GOD	
Scripture verses	1 John 1:5-10
High level key topic	Honesty keeps us close to God. God will forgive us when we confess our sins

SCRIPTURAL LESSON NARRATIVE

Honesty is choosing to be truthful in what you say and do. Can you be dishonest by not saying something? Sure. Sometimes by being silent and withholding information you can be more dishonest than times when you open your mouth and lie. The problem with dishonesty and not telling the truth is that you can hurt others, yourself and cause others to lose their trust in you. That can be difficult to earn back. And often like the boy who cried wolf it can create difficulties for you.

When we are honest people learn they can trust us. When they trust us they may give us more responsibility, more freedom and independence and more opportunities. When we are dishonest the opposite happens and they monitor us more closely, skeptical about whether we can be trusted. From the beginning God has made and kept all His promises. We should do the same.

Sometimes lies happen because we are afraid if we tell the truth we will get in trouble. So we try to hide the truth. But we cannot hide the truth from God. Because we know this it creates a sickening feeling inside us during the time we try to hide it. That feeling will only go away once you are honest with God. When you try to hide it, it keeps you separated from God. You tend to not want to communicate with God about anything because you know that issue is like a cloud over your head and you would rather try to ignore it and forget it than to talk with God about it. But once you do talk to God about it He forgives you and you will feel better. It will bring you close to God once again. You will feel better about it. You will feel relieved to get it off your chest. And God will help you through any problems that arise from telling the truth. Telling God the truth is for our benefit. It shows Him that we still believe in Him. It shows that we are trying to do the right thing. It shows Him we can own up to our mistakes. It shows Him we are ready for more responsibility. It shows Him we are starting to grow and mature into an adult. As long as we try to hide things from God it will hold back our spiritual and emotional growth. Talk to God. When you hold things back you are separated from Him and bad things can happen when you are not in continual communication with God.

MATCH THE EXPLANATION
WITH THE APOLOGETICS ISSUE

ISSUE	EXPLANATION
Problem of evil and suffering	Small changes do occur over time. But no evidence that the changes could create different species. Science shows almost all animals created approximately at the same time.
Trinity	But many things are unseen: beauty, love, consciousness. Yet we believe in those. If evidence points to something unseen, it is not irrational to believe it exists.
Big Bang caused the universe	God knows in their hearts if they would have accepted Him.
Life was created randomly from nonliving chemicals	Nonsensical statement. Not logically possible so it doesn't require an answer.
God is in control or we have freedom to choose	Adam and Even had many sons and daughters and so Cain and Seth had choices over a long period of time.
Was Jesus really resurrected	The Bible allows for old or youth earth depending on the correct definition of "day" in Genesis.
Miracles are not possible	God gave us free will. Original sin. Some evil is created by Satan. God has reasons to allow some suffering. God creates good from evil.
Science and the Bible disagree	But creation of the universe and first life do not have reasonable explanations from science. Evidence points to a Supreme Being.
Where do our morals come from	Jesus predicted His own violent death. If correct Islam is false because they say He didn't day. If not correct, Islam is false because that would make Him a false prophet and they say He was a great prophet.
Is evolution true	No evidence of a common ancestor of humans. Genetics traces humans back to single male and female 5000 to 7500 years ago.
Science says the universe is billions of years old	But what caused the Big Bang? Evidence to points a supreme being.
Science says we are descended from apes	Not enough time for random chance to create life. Life contains information, which only comes from an intelligent source. Evidence more likely that an all intelligent source created life.
All religions are true	Can't be so because they contradict each other.
The Bible is myth and legend and can't be trusted	He is both. Fully God but added a human form.

ISSUE	EXPLANATION
It's not rational to have faith in the unseen	People who reject Him have made their own decision. They can accept and find salvation.
God doesn't exist	The gospels were written within 40 years of Jesus by reliable eyewitnesses to the resurrection. 5700 NT Greek copies agree with 99% accuracy.
Maybe Islam is true	Tomb was empty. Over 500 eyewitnesses saw Him.
What about people who never hear about Jesus	If we agree some things are right or wrong, must be a moral law giver outside of us. Points to God as source of morals.
Why would God send people to hell	Evidence from science points to God, such as creation of the universe and of first life.
Can God make a rock so heavy He can't lift it	God exists in three persons: father, son and Holy Spirit
If only Adam and Eve, where did all the other people come from	Both. We have free will but God knows what we will do and created a plan before time began using that knowledge.
Is Jesus man or God	It only seems that way. Science could be wrong, or we may have misinterpreted some scripture, or a bit of both.

WHAT ABOUT THOSE WHO NEVER HEAR ABOUT GOD?

One of the areas that are difficult for us as Christians is to understand salvation and how it works. Before Jesus was born, people must have been judged by how they responded to their knowledge of God. Did they pray, try to obey the laws, and so forth. Once Jesus was born, salvation was based on hearing and accepting Jesus as Savior and Lord and following Him.

But it is a fair and confusing question to ask, what about those who never hear about Jesus or God or ever see a Bible? Here are some examples:

- A Muslim boy grows up in the Middle East and is forbidden from hearing, studying or learning about anything but Islam

- A retarded or otherwise handicapped person who cannot reason and understand as a normal person

- A person who lives in a remote country, area or jungle who has never been exposed to any religion

- A child, baby, or very young person who dies before they are capable of understanding language and learning

Are these people doomed? Are they automatically saved? What about them?

I'm going to give you a couple answers.

1. The heavens declare the glory of God. Psalm 19:1. This passage indicates we can know God even if no one preaches the gospel to us. Let me go further. The Apostle Paul writes in Romans 1:18-23: no man is without an excuse. He is saying it is evident that God exists merely by looking at the world around us. So I believe what this means is that each of us looks at the natural world and can see it as a sign of God. Some may stop there and reject it and they may be lost if they never become seekers of the knowledge of God. But if they do become seekers, God will continue to provide knowledge to them and they may one day find salvation in Christ.

2. God is omniscient. He reads their hearts, and knows what if they would accept Christ if they did hear the gospel. We call this God's middle knowledge, His ability to know what we will do in any circumstance.

For me these are the best answers. I believe God measures us partly on what we know and partly on what is in our hearts. If He knows how many stars are in the skies and how many hairs on each of our heads, and what we will say before we say it, is it any stretch to say He knows what we would do in any situation?

Also, I believe we will find that not every Christian will be in heaven and not every atheist or Muslim will be in hell. What someone says on the outside is not necessarily what they believe on the inside. Please recognize this and when we say that a person must accept Christ to have salvation, we must also understand that only God knows for sure if they did and if they would. It is not our place to judge whether they are doomed or saved. We can only know what is required for salvation but not know if someone obtains it or not.

Let's pray for all those who never hear of Christ and ask that God search their hearts and help them find Him anyway.

ARE MIRACLES POSSIBLE?

Throughout the Bible miracles were done to prove God's power, to increase the faith of believers, and provide evidence for nonbelievers. But science says miracles are impossible because by definition a miracle is supernatural and something that happens outside the laws of nature. But they don't believe there is anything outside of nature so they deny miracles. Since the Bible is based on many miracles, science says that the Bible is wrong.

Miracles are basically a disruption of a natural law of physics. So when Jesus tells a paralyzed man to get up and walk, that is physically not possible and is a miracle. When Jesus raised Lazarus from the dead and raised himself, when he made blind men see, when He walked on water, turned water into wine, calmed a terrible storm, turned a small fish basket into food for 5,000, and the many more miracles, science says these were not possible.

There are two reasons why science is wrong.

1. Science is wrong because there were hundreds to thousands of witnesses to the miracles of Jesus. No one ever came forward to dispute the scriptures and claim the miracles were false. There were still many alive when the scriptures were recorded so why did they not come forward, since the Romans were offering great rewards to anyone who could help them stamp out Christianity? Because the miracles were true. So they are a historical record. We had lessons where we showed the evidence that the Bible is true and historically reliable. So miracles are recorded like many other facts and they are true. They are not made up.

2. Science is wrong because the two greatest miracles that have ever happened cannot be explained by science and yet we know they have happened – the creation of the universe and the creation of life. The scientific theory called "the Big Bang" explains that the universe had a beginning, which the Bible acknowledges. But the Big Bang theory explains that something was created out of nothing. Before the universe was created there was no time, no matter and no space. So how could nothing create something? They have no explanation but know that it happened. The explanation is God. The Bible tells us that through Jesus the entire universe was created. So that proves that miracles can happen.

As for life, science also cannot explain how first life was created. Understand that the theory of evolution has to do with how things changed over time after life was formed and has nothing to say about first life. Theories have been stated that it was random chance of the right non-living chemicals forming to create life but it is proven to be mathematically impossible. They have stated a theory that somehow the chemicals had self-replication ability and created it. But we know that RNA and proteins are two requirements for life. These are chemical mixtures within a cell. But RNA cannot be formed without proteins and proteins cannot be formed without RNA, so that means they both had to be formed at the same time. Scientifically that is not possible and there is no explanation. That is a miracle. We know that God created life on the sixth day.

BIBLE BOWL CONTEST

100 pts each for first answer; 50 points for second team answer if first team is wrong

1. Is the universe eternal or did it have a beginning?

    It had a beginning

2. A word we use to call the Father, Son, and Holy Spirit together?

    Trinity

3. Adam and Eve lived over 900 years old. True or False?

    True

4. After the flood, God changed people's average life span to how many years?

    120 years

5. He was over 9 feet tall.

    Goliath

6. He wrote most of the Psalms.

    King David

7. He wrote most of the Proverbs.

    King Solomon

8. He led the Israelites out of the wilderness over a period of 40 years.

    Moses

9. He was in the burning furnace along with Meshach, Shadrach, and Abednego.

    Jesus

10. Spell one of the above correctly.

    see above

11. Describe apologetics or give a definition defense, defending Christianity

12. What is a prophecy prediction, message from God

13. The famous characters of the Bible are role models for Christians. True or False?

    False

14. Which famous character of the Bible is a role model for Christians?

    Jesus

15. Explain how God could justify killing all Egyptian first born males.

> *God is all-just but patient. 9 plagues were sent to convince the Pharaoh but he refused. God is sovereign and delivers judgment where needed to accomplish His plan.*

16. Explain how God could allow mass killings by the Jews over the people in the land of milk and honey.

> *God is all-just but patient. He waited 400 years for the Canaanites to worship Him but they worshipped idols and practiced horrific baby-burning sacrifices to their god Molech. Eventually God delivered judgment to complete His plan with the Israelites.*

17. He wrote Genesis.

> *Moses*

18. He wrote Luke.

> *Luke*

19. He wrote Acts.

> *Luke*

20. He was Paul's assistant and a doctor.

> *Luke*

21. He was Peter's assistant.

> *Mark*

22. How many total books in the bible?

> *66*

23. How many books in the NT?

> *27*

24. How many authors wrote all the books in the NT?

> *9*

25. He became a King after being born of David and Bathsheba.

> *King Solomon*

26. Recite John 3:16.

> *God so loved the world He gave His only Son that whoever believes in Him shall not die but have life forever.*

27. The name of this great tower built by a nonbelieving king.

> *Tower of Babel*

28. Who were the two Sauls described in the Bible?

> *King Saul and the Apostle Paul*

29. Scientists say miracles are impossible. But name 1 of 2 greatest that has happened they can't explain.

    Creation of universe, creation of first life

30. Why Jesus was sent to earth?

    Save us from our sins

31. How many days after Jesus was dead did he rise?

    3 days

32. The reason we are all born with a sinful nature.

    the Fall, inherited from Adam

33. The reason the universe exists.

    an all-powerful, eternal, timeless cause - God

34. What does the name Esau mean?

    Reddish, ruddy

35. What does the name Jesus mean?

    the Lord saves

36. What does the name Immanuel mean?

    God with us

37. The town Jesus was born in?

    Bethlehem

38. The town Jesus was raised in?

    Nazareth

39. How old was Jesus when he died?

    33 or 30

40. What AD stands for?

    Ante diluvium, commonly referred to as '*after death*'

41. What BC stands for?

    Before Christ

42. What does intercede mean or intercession?

    Come between/stand up for; Jesus intercedes for us with the Father

43. What are the ABC's of becoming a Christian?

    Admit you are a sinner; Believe Jesus is God; Confess He is your Lord and Savior

44. Why must we confess our sins when they happen?

> *To repair the separation from God that a sin causes; to recognize/admit when we do something wrong; to receive God's forgiveness*

45. Why must we forgive others?

> *Because God forgives us and we are not greater than Him*

46. He killed Goliath?

> *David*

47. The weapon that killed Goliath?

> *sling and stone*

48. What is the Great Commission?

> *Matt. 28:16-20: Go forth and spread the gospel, baptizing everyone in the name of the Father, Son and Holy Spirit*

49. Explain why all religions can't be true they contradict in their core beliefs.

> *(law of noncontradiction)*

50. What was Paul's name before he became a believer?

> *Saul*

51. The name of the Jewish leader who had Jesus arrested and crucified?

> *Caiaphas*

52. The name of the Roman leader who washed his hands of Jesus' crucifixion?

> *Pilate*

53. The name of the torture that Jesus endured on the cross?

> *crucifixion*

54. Which is a miracle? – creation of universe, your aunt recovers from cancer, a tree falls and barely misses your car.

> *could be all but first one for sure*

55. All religions lead to heaven. True or False?

> *True*

56. Everyone lives forever. True or False?

> *True, either in heaven or hell*

57. The only religion that believes Jesus was God, died for our sins, and was resurrected?

> *Christianity*

58. What should we do because Jesus saved us?

   believe in Him and follow His teachings

59. Name two major prophets?

   Isaiah, Jeremiah, Ezekiel, Daniel

60. He predicted to the exact day, hundreds of years in advance, when Jesus would ride into Jerusalem on Palm Sunday?

   Daniel; Daniel 9:24, 483 years in advance

61. Why do we celebrate Easter?

   the resurrection

62. Was Jesus God or man or both?

   both

63. Why didn't Jesus save Himself from being crucified?

   To fulfill God's plan to save us from our sins

64. The name of the Garden Jesus prayed in the night of his arrest?

   Gethsemane

65. While Jesus was praying in the Garden the night of his arrest, what did his disciples do?

   fall asleep

66. He denied Jesus 3 times?

   Peter

67. He betrayed Jesus for 30 pieces of silver?

   Judas

68. What Judas did after he betrayed Jesus?

   hanged himself

69. How many original disciples were there?

   12

70. The difference between an apostle and a disciple?

   a disciple is a follower of Jesus; an apostle is a disciple who witnessed the resurrected Jesus and was given the power to do miracles

71. How many appearances of Jesus within 40 days after he was resurrected?

   12

72. How many people saw the resurrected Jesus? – 10, 50, over 500?

   over 500

73. Give 5 names for God/Jesus.

Immanuel, Lord, Savior, Almighty God, Wonderful Counselor, other descriptive titles

74. Mr. Kevin's last name?

Dawson

75. My last name?

Griffin

76. How many days and nights was the great flood?

40

77. Why were Noah and his family spared?

Noah was the only righteous person left

78. Who wrote Revelation?

John

79. Do we have the original of the Bible? Yes or No?

No

80. What do we call the 7 year period in Revelation when 21 judgments/disasters occur on the earth?

Tribulation

81. What happens after the Tribulation period?

Armageddon; second coming of Jesus; Jesus destroys the armies against Israel and wipes out evil

82. Name in order the books of the OT.

50 pts refer to Bible

83. Name in order the books of the NT.

50 pts refer to Bible

84. What is the first name of each person on the other team per your class?

85. What is the first name of each person on your team per your class?

86. We can earn our way into heaven by following the commandments all our lives. True or False?

False

87. What natural disruption happened when Jesus was put on the cross?

eclipse

88. What natural disruption happened when Jesus gave his last breath?

earthquake

89. He bought a tomb for Jesus and asked for his body to bury Him.

Joseph of Arimathea

90. The first people to see the empty tomb were women. True or False?

True

91. What did Jesus say about the Roman guards while he was on the cross before He died?

God forgive them for they know not what they do.

92. Name 3 proofs that Jesus was God.

prophecies, virgin birth, miracles, He said He was I AM and admitted He was the Christ, admitted He was Messiah, asked for worship, forgave sins

93. What was Matthew's job?

Tax collector

94. Jesus mainly preached to the Jews, but Paul mainly preached to whom?

gentiles

95. What did Joseph's brothers do to him threw him in a pit?

sold him into slavery

96. Muslims say Jesus was only a good teacher and prophet, not God. What is wrong with believing that?

Since He claimed He was good, then if Muslims are right He was a false prophet. If Muslims are wrong, then He was God and they are wrong and Islam is false either way.

97. What was the name of the honey like wafer that rained from heaven for the Jews in the wilderness?

manna

98. What does manna mean? what is it?

99. He had all the soldiers shout and the walls of what city came tumbling down?

Jericho

100. Who was he?

Joshua

101. Give me a reason why God allows evil.

free will; prepare and build our character; to do good from it; prepare us for the next world to come; show us courage, compassion, etc.

102. Give me another reason why God allows evil.

    see above

103. What does God promise He will do about evil.

    destroy it one day

104. What do we call the special sign the early Christians used that looked like a fish?

    ichthus

105. Why did they use it to know if someone was a Christian instead of risking exposure or imprisonment?

    if it was a spy or Roman soldier

106. Draw it like a fish outline – one vertical line, partial infinity symbol on its side connected to the line

107. His brothers threw him in a well and tried to kill him but he escaped and later was 2nd in charge for Egypt.

    Joseph

108. In the story of the prodigal son, what does prodigal mean?

    Wasteful, reckless

109. Name 3 ways you can be involved to tell others about Jesus.

    invite to Sunday School, give them a bible, share the gospel message that Jesus died for them

110. What are 3 of the key elements of a model prayer?

    Ask forgiveness, give thanks, pray for others, pray for what you need, let God's will be done

111. What would you say if someone told you that you that there is no God?

    Ask them for evidence; why do you believe that? What did you study that proved that?

112. Evolution explains how life was first created. True or False

    False, only describes what they think happened after first life was created

113. This 3 letter scientific word is in every organism that is or was alive.

    DNA

114. What is the special thing called in all living things that is like an instruction manual?

    DNA

115. God created heaven and earth in how many days?

    6, He rested/ceased on day 7

116. Adam and Eve's son who killed his brother?

    Cain

117. Jesus was born of what race/nationality?

    Jewish

118. Did Jesus have any brothers and sisters?

    Yes several of both, technical half-brothers and half-sisters

119. What was the name of the well-known brother of Jesus who wrote a NT book?

    James

120. Adam and Eve had Cain and Abel and Seth – where did their wives come from?

    (delicate, sensitive discussion); from nieces and cousins and generally their relatives

121. What was the name of the famous preaching Jesus did on the Mount of Olives?

    Beatitudes; Sermon on the Mount

122. Name one of the fruits of the Spirit as Paul described.

    love, joy, peace, patience, kindness, goodness, faithfulness, 23 gentleness, self-control

123. Esther was selected as queen for what main reason?

    beauty

124. The 10 commandments can divide into 2 types – first 4 about whom? second 6 about whom?

    God; others

125. Name the 10 commandments.

    no other gods; no idols; no swearing; remember the Sabbath; honor your parents; don't murder, commit adultery, steal or lie or covet

126. Where will Christians be when the Tribulation period of Revelation begins?

    Debatable; either raptured and with Jesus; or either dead or alive waiting for His return

127. When Jesus returns next, how will we know?

    trumpet and He will be seen in the clouds

128. Why does God create prophecies?

    Display His power; provide evidence so we will believe; give a message to the people

129. Has a Biblical prophecy ever been proven wrong? Yes or No?

    No

130. **What name did God tell Moses to use to call Himself?**

   I AM

131. **What does "I am" indicate or mean?**

   the self-existing one

132. **What does it mean when the Bible says God is a jealous God?**

   He does not want us to worship other gods; it is an expression in human emotions terms

133. **Why is it not enough for salvation to just acknowledge that Jesus is God?**

   The demons recognize He is God but do not follow Him

134. **Since all religions teach some core principles, do all religions worship the same God?**

   No they differ in all key core doctrinal beliefs so they cannot all be true. Examine the evidence to see what is true or false.

135. **All roads lead to heaven. True or False?**

   False

136. **It's okay for a Christian to not believe in heaven or hell. True or False?**

   False, it is not Biblical

137. **How is the Bible different than other religions' scriptures?**

   Based on historical record and eyewitness testimony

138. **The Big Bang is a scientific proof that God does not exist. True or False?**

   False

139. **The average age of many in the OT Genesis book was 900 years old. True or False?**

   True

140. **Why did God change our maximum life span to 120 years?**

   to prevent us from doing more evil

141. **What was the number one cause of death at the time of the Noah flood?**

   murder

142. **What is the number one cause of death in the world today if we include abortion (consider appropriateness)?**

   murder

143. **Why is abortion not an acceptable principle for Christians (consider appropriateness)?**

   It is murder; Lev. 17:11 and Psalm 51:5 (we have a soul and are human)

144. What is the difference between murder and kill?

> *Murder is killing innocents; killing could be self-defense or justifiable war or justifiable execution*

145. If you have a friend who is not a Christian what should you do?

> *Share the gospel; invite them to Sunday School; ask them if they would like to learn about Jesus*

146. The NT is historically reliable. True or False?

> *True*

147. Jesus claimed to be God. True or False?

> *True, directly and indirectly*

148. Name 3 reasons we know Jesus died and was resurrected?

> *Eyewitnesses, changed behavior of disciples, empty tomb, rapid expansion of Christianity*

149. What caused the apostles to go from being timid and weak to fearless and bold?

> *Their understanding and belief in the meaning of the resurrection*

150. Jesus never sinned. True or False?

> *True*

151. If Jesus is really God, then how could the devil have tempted Him?

> *Tempted in his human nature only*

152. When Jesus was 12 and stayed in the Temple, he sinned because he disobeyed His parents – True or False sort of yes and no.

> *He didn't really disobey but should have told them where He would be*

153. There were times when Jesus' family thought He was crazy. True or False?

> *True*

154. What is the Islam/Muslim scripture called?

> *Qur'an; Koran*

155. Muslims believe Jesus was a good teacher and prophet. True or False?

> *True*

156. Muslims believe Jesus was God. True or False

> *False*

157. Muslims believe Jesus died on the cross. True or False?

> *False*

158. Is it a good or bad idea to increase church membership by removing offensive concepts such as the cross, heaven, hell, saved, unsaved, sin, repentance? And why or why not?

  Bad, this is prosperity preaching and ignores that we are sinners; provides false understanding because we will all have hard times

159. Jesus taught that pride is a sin. True or False?

  True

160. In the story of the rich young ruler, does Jesus teach we have to give away all our money and follow Him to have eternal life?. True or False?

  no that is an exaggeration to make a point that it is hard to be a believer when you have wealth which becomes all important and an idol

161. Why does God forbid worshiping false idols?

  Because they are false and will lead to destruction

162. What are 2 false idols people may worship today?

  Wealth, power, status, etc.

163. Moses parted the waters of what Sea?

  Red Sea

164. Moses died before crossing what river?

  Jordan River

165. Where did Moses grow up?

  Pharaoh's palace

166. Why did Moses flee from Egypt?

  he killed an Egyptian who was beating up a Jew

167. Why can't there be more than one all-powerful God?

  by definition there can only be one who is the most powerful otherwise the other one would be all-powerful

168. How can you explain that we have free will but God knows who will be saved before time began?

  God is omniscient so He knows the end from the beginning and knew our free choices when He set His master plan before He created

169. Can evolution explain how life began?

  No, it only deals with the assumption of first life and how they believe all species came about

170. Who came up with the theory of evolution?

  Charles Darwin

171. Critics of the Bible say there are many errors – what kind of errors are there?

primarily copying errors; some minor word changes for better understanding

172. The old testament was written in two languages – name one.

Hebrew, Aramaic

173. Name the other.

see above

174. The new testament was written in what language.

Greek

175. What happens to people who do not accept Jesus as Lord?

their sin condemns them to hell

176. Do we need to be baptized to be saved?

No

177. What is baptism for?

announce your faith to others

178. What core principle of Christianity is the key difference with all other religions?

Jesus is God

179. Is it possible for two things that teach opposites to both be true?

No

180. Truth is dependent on your view of reality. True or False?

No, what corresponds to reality

181. Truth can be different for different people?

No, it is the same for everyone, everywhere, at all times (in the same sense and time)

182. Why is the definition of science wrong?

It is the search for natural causes but that logically omits unnatural/supernatural causes and prevents consideration of God

183. Name one way Jesus claimed to be God.

He said "I AM", admitted He was the Christ as His trial, said He was the Messiah with the woman at the well, said He and the Father were One, forgave sins, accepted worship

184. Another see above

185. Another see above

186. Name a way Jesus proved He was God.

predicted and fulfilled through His resurrection

187. Jesus fulfilled how many old testament prophecies – 19, 50, 100?

about 100

188. How do you get access to the Holy Spirit?

He indwells you when you accept Christ

189. What is one thing that the Holy Spirit does for us?

Helps us make Godly decisions, convicts us of sin, convicts us to be saved, protects us from some evils

190. Once you are a Christian, you can never be taken away from God. True or False?

True

191. Once you are a Christian, you can never be tempted by the devil. True or False?

False

192. Once you are a Christian, you no longer sin. True or False?

False

193. Once you are a Christian, you are transformed and reborn. True or False?

True

194. Explain what grace is?

A free gift from God

195. God requires that we stop sinning before grace is given. True or False?

False

196. Without faith there is no salvation. True or False?

True

197. What happens when Jesus conquers all enemies at the battle of Armageddon?

He destroys evil then reigns on earth for 1000 years

198. How is apologetics important helps us understand why we believe?

helps us to know Christianity is true; helps us address objections and criticisms from others

199. When you hear people say negative things about God, Christianity, and the Bible, will you believe it?

No

200. What will you do?

Ask them why they believe that; what information or research made them come to that conclusion; share a couple points or questions that point to God; share the gospel

The following are typical questions you may encounter and should be prepared to answer. In case some of the curriculum lessons do not cover a few of these or go too deep, I have provided some short answers or suggestions to review. This material can be used to fill in gaps when scriptural or apologetics lessons are not available or to mix up the format with something a little different. Mix a few of these in here and there as regular discussion items.

1. Were there dinosaurs when Adam and Eve lived?

   - *No, dinosaurs went extinct 66 million years before humans were created. This occurred in the earlier part of day six in Genesis. (be prepared to address young earth/old earth at some point and explain that the Bible actually supports an old earth or a young earth whichever is found to be true ultimately)*

2. Where did all the people come from if only Cain and Abel were the children?

   - *Actually the Bible mentions a third son Seth and says that Adam and Eve had other children. It is a sensitive fact to discuss that until after the flood, God allowed marriage between cousins, nieces, nephews, etc. After about 48 generations God laid down a new law prohibiting such. This corresponds with our science today that shows birth defects can occur after about 48 generations. God already knew that.*

3. How did they get all the animals on the ark?

   - *If you read Genesis carefully, it talks about certain 'kinds' that entered the ark. So insects and fish and other related species like of the cat family for example were not necessary to be boarded. The ark in its recorded measurements was large enough to hold about 16,000 to 50,000 animals but perhaps only about 2,000 were needed (equivalent space of 569 railroad cars).*

4. Did people really live to 900 years old?

   - *Yes, Methuselah was the oldest and lived to 969 years old. Adam and Eve both lived to about 920 years old. This is best answered by a supernovae explosion called Vela that occurred after the flood and sent destructive cosmic radiation pouring onto earth and eventually limited human life spans. More specifically, Gen. 6:3 explains that after the flood sometime, God limited human life spans to 120 years so we could not do so much evil. Genetic mutations may also play a major role over the millennia.*

5. Are some of the miracles just stories, like Jonah and the whale?

- *No, you cannot cherry pick teachings from the Bible. The Bible is inerrant in all its teachings. Certainly there are literary tools used such as metaphors, poetry, exaggeration, apocalyptic descriptions, simile, anthropomorphism, and many others. But if the teaching is not part of one of those literary styles then the teaching must be regarded as true. Also, Jesus made reference to Jonah so that ensures it was a fact.*

6. Our teacher said evolution is not true – is that right?

- *Well it depends on the definition of evolution. If it is meant in its broadest term which means things change over time then yes it is true. If it is meant in a Darwinian evolutionary paradigm such that they claim all species were created through evolution then no the evidence for that is scant and negligible if not outright non-existent.*

7. Our teacher said the earth is 7200 yrs. old – is that right?

- *According to science, no, it is about 4.57 billion years old. From the perspective of the Bible, it supports a young earth or old earth due to the multiple definitions and uses of the word 'yom' which is Hebrew for day. It allows for a twelve hour daylight period, 24 hour period, part of a 24 hour period, or indefinite longer period of time. So whatever is the correct answer the Bible can support either. This is an interesting but unimportant debate from the standpoint of Christianity but is a delicate matter when discussing with nonbelievers so a neutral position is preferable.*

8. My Muslim friend said we are blasphemers – what is that?

- *A blasphemer is someone who refutes or denies God or specifically the Holy Spirit. The Muslim claim is due to the Christian doctrine of the Trinity. The Bible shows that God is one nature in three persons. Muslims misunderstand this and claim we believe in three Gods, which is not the case.*

9. My aunt is a Buddhist – is she going to hell?

- *Only God truly knows the answer to this. According to the Bible and specifically Jesus (John 14:6; 1 John 4:3, 2:22), He is the only way to the Father and eternal life. But there is debate about those who have not heard the gospel message and it is an unsettled question whether direct knowledge of the gospel is required. Clearly if someone rejects the gospel message they doom themselves. But if they have some knowledge or perhaps God reads their heart and knows what they would do if presented the gospel, those may be possibilities. The best thing to do is present the gospel to hear and help her believe.*

10. The big bang is not true right?

- *The science is quite conclusive that there is such a thing as the Big Bang. However, it is misunderstood. The Big Bang is not the cause of the universe but rather a description of how it began. It still requires a cause and God is the most likely answer because whatever created the universe was all powerful, eternal and timeless. The Big Bang does not disprove God.*

11. I heard they found Noah's Ark. Does that prove Christianity is true?

   – *There is an ongoing claim that the Ark was found in Turkey in the mountains of Ararat. However, further expeditions are required to validate the claim. The Ark's existence itself lends credence to the truth of Christianity but does not prove Christianity itself. The resurrection is the needed proof.*

12. Was Jesus praying to himself in the garden when he prayed to the Father?

   – *Technically no. Jesus had two natures: human and divine. He prayed in his human form to the Father, who is a person of the Trinity as Jesus is. The three persons of the Trinity have different roles and responsibilities. The Father is the master planner; the Son is the one who executes the plan; the Holy Spirit is the one who applies the plan to each of us.*

13. Did God create evil or did Satan?

   – *God did not create evil. He created free will for humans and sometimes they make bad decisions. Satan does create some evils that exist. Evil is a privation (lack) of good. It is based on sinful human decisions in some cases. In other cases it comes from natural disasters which possibly are influenced by Satan.*

14. Why doesn't God kill Satan?

   – *Eventually God will throw Satan into the eternal Lake of Fire after Jesus destroys evil. God could kill Satan but the best answer is that His plan for humanity and our redemption involved not only Jesus but Satan as well. It could be that Satan and evil are not just tolerated but used to help humans develop character and values such as compassion, courage, empathy, caring and love. These traits may be necessary to prepare us for the world to come after our physical death.*

15. Why didn't God keep Satan out of Eden if He knew what would happen?

   – *A similar answer to the above. Satan also had free will and God used Satan and his horrific acts for the good of humankind and to develop us into the best version of who we can be.*

16. If heaven is a perfect paradise with no evil and suffering, why didn't God make it on earth instead?

   – *I often ask myself this question. Perhaps the best answer is that humans need considerable character development and understanding of evil and suffering in order to prepare us for the perfect world in paradise. Perhaps we could not appreciate the horror of evil and suffering without first experiencing it.*

17. If God knew Adam would sin why did He allow it?

- *God gave Adam free will. It could be that the best possible world to prepare us for heaven is one where free will exists rather than creating robotic humans who do exactly as God wants. Perhaps we learn best through suffering and sin.*

18. Does God get angry like the Bible says?

- *Not in the way humans do. This is an example of the writer documenting his perspective about God's nature in human terms. But God is not affected by human emotions or reactions. If it were so it would be somewhat of a denial of his omniscience and omnipotence. In other words, if God knows someone will do something that He does not want, He could have accounted for that when He created. God cannot be surprised so whatever happens He knows will happen and cannot be angered by it or affected by it in a reactive way.*

19. Why does the Bible say God hated Esau?

- *The correct translation for the Hebrew word used is better understood as God loved Esau less. In essence, God preferred Jacob to implement His plan for Israel and all nations and people.*

20. Do we come from apes?

- *No, there is no identified common ancestor for apes and humans. It is simply assumed by scientists because they believe that is how evolution works. But God created humans as a special creation from the dust. Anthropologists incorrectly make assumptions based on Darwinian evolution. They claim that the similarity of body forms and fossils show that apes are similar to us so there must be a common ancestor for apes and humans. This is really part of the evolution debate. Their claim that our DNA is 95% the same is more readily attributable to a common design. Our DNA is actually closer to that of a chicken than an ape. But no one claims we descended from a common ancestor of chickens and humans. Also, it is proven that from a language perspective apes are unable to develop language and sounds as humans can and it is actually birds such as ravens and crows and specifically parrots that are closer to humans than apes in this capability. So it is infeasible that apes and humans descended from a common ancestor. But no one claims that we descended from birds instead.*

21. I heard that Jesus appears in the OT too, is that right?

- *Yes we believe so. Such an appearance is called a theophany. While in His divine nature Jesus may have taken on the form of a human and appeared in instances where referenced as the Angel of the Lord, the Commander of God's army, wrestling with Jacob perhaps, or in the burning furnace with Meshach, Shadrach and Abednego.*

22. What about the OT people who never knew Jesus, are they saved?

- *This is a difficult question and part of the general question, "What about those who do not hear the gospel?" I believe the best and most straightforward answer to the question is that God is omniscient and knows every heart and what decision every person would make in every circumstance. So He knows what every person would choose if presented the gospel. Also, for the OT characters, they may have had knowledge of the Messiah but not of Jesus in particular so either God knows their heart or perhaps He provides more information to those who seek Him until they are saved, or otherwise we just do not know.*

23. I heard there were some prophecies that did not come true, is that right?

- *No, every prophecy has either been proven correct or will be proven correct in the future for some yet to be fulfilled. Nonbelievers have tried for centuries to dispute some claims but either they base their claims on false assumptions, false information, or merely deny based on a denial of the possibility of miracles and God's existence.*

24. If I do badly after I am saved, will I still go to heaven?

- *This is a controversial question about salvation within Christianity. There is sufficient scripture to indicate that once we are in Christ, He never loses us. So it is unlikely that we can lose our salvation. Everyone sins so we must recognize our sin and ask God's forgiveness and we are placed back in a right relationship with Him again.*

25. We learned the abc's of salvation, is that all it takes?

- *Yes but it must be a sincere prayer and belief. Remember that God is all-knowing and knows your heart so you cannot trick Him. It is not sufficient to merely say the words. It must be a real experience. So admit you are a sinner; Believe Jesus is God; Confess He is your Savior.*

26. Are Muslims terrorists?

- *There are different categories of terrorists and some are not Muslims. But if the question is about ISIS and other Islamic terrorists then yes they are Muslims. It is a contested and controversial issue. Moderate Muslims and some liberal politicians and religious figures may say that those terrorists do not represent Islam. However, it is a fact that they are following what the Qur'an states about violent jihad (holy war) and that they are mimicking what Mohammed did in his time.*

27. Will Christians suffer during the tribulation time?

- *This is also controversial within the Christian community. Some believe in a pre-tribulation rapture where Jesus appears in the clouds and Christians are called up to Him and spared the devastation of the tribulation. Others believe that such appearance of Jesus happens post-tribulation and that*

Christians must endure the wrath of God during the tribulation. It appears that the pre-tribulation rapture has lost some support and that the scriptural support for it is very dubious and requires assumptions not evidenced in the scripture itself.

28. Was Jesus wrong when He said this generation will not pass until I return?

 - *There are several passages amongst a couple of the gospels that discuss this and the actual scripture is mixed across two topics. On the one hand, Jesus was originally asked a question about the temple and it is likely this answer about the generation not passing before it witnessed such was referring to that event. However, He also spoke of the end times and His reappearance and in another scripture He answered the question and said that "some here" will not pass until they see Him in His glory. The next passages in scripture describe the "transfiguration" appearance with several of His disciples and Elijah and Moses so that may be what was referenced as well. Another answer that some prefer is that "generation" refers to the church age. But it is clear that He could not be wrong because although in his human nature He did not access all His divine knowledge, it is unthinkable that He could make a false claim. Unfortunately, there are some people who have even lost their faith because they believe Jesus was wrong and was referring to his second coming in the near future after those passages. This emphasizes the need for careful study of scripture and commentaries and not making rash decisions without investigation.*

29. Will we have bodies in heaven?

 - *The Bible is not clear on this subject as far as I can understand. It could be that we are only spirits in heaven, or perhaps there is some "avatar-like" representation of us, or that we only communicate via thoughts in heaven. Since the Bible mentions our bodies rise and are transformed at the second coming and world resurrection, it seems unlikely that we have a third interim body while in heaven before the second coming.*

30. Where do we go right after we die?

 - *Saved Christians' soul/spirit is immediately in heaven with Jesus. Our body remains on earth until the second coming and world resurrection.*

31. Are Catholics part of Christianity?

 - *Yes because they believe Jesus is God and that He offered salvation through His sacrifice of bearing the penalty of our sins. There is ongoing controversy about some of their beliefs and practices which contradict Protestantism that are nagging issues. They believe Mary was sinless and pray to/ through her, they allow human priests to forgive sins, they deny that faith is sufficient for salvation without good works and that actually the sacraments are required for salvation among other lesser known differences.*

32. My neighbors are Mormons and said they are Christians. Is that right?

- *No Mormonism is a cult, an aberration and perversion of Christianity. It is a man-made religion born of a human who had a vision and distorted scripture and Christian doctrine to form his own religion. There are many false beliefs and denials of key doctrine such as the Trinity and nature of God and Jesus and man. The membership is failing and is making a desperate attempt to normalize their beliefs by saying and promoting the idea that they are part of Christianity.*

33. Why do Muslims and terrorists want to kill us?

- *Not all Muslims are terrorists and not all Muslims want to kill us. But for those who do it is because there are 100 passages in the Qur'an (Islam's scripture) that call their believers to external jihad (violent holy war). The jihad is against Christians and Jews in particular but anyone who is a non-believer of Islam also, including some Muslims who follow the Sunni sect of Islam or who may not believe in external jihad.*

34. I heard it is legal to kill babies before they are born, how can that be?

- *(address this topic as you see appropriate for your church situation). Yes it is actually true that in 1973 the Supreme Court passed a law that referred to the actual case called Roe v. Wade to allow babies in the womb to be destroyed at the discretion of the mother and perhaps father. It is a blasphemy against God and non-biblical, enacted mostly for convenience, and is the same as murder. 70 million babies have been murdered/aborted in America since that time. Perhaps one day the Supreme Court will consist of conservative justices who will overturn this ruling.*

35. Somebody told me the Bible was like fairy tales or myth and legend, is that right?

- *No not at all. The Bible is the only religious scripture that is based on historical record and documented by historical persons who were eyewitnesses to events. There are some parables and exaggerations and other literary tools that extend beyond historicity in some cases, but all the teachings of the Bible are inerrant. This belief about fairy tales comes from the false idea that the Bible was created hundreds of years after Jesus so that it is composed of mere myth and legends with no provable historical origination.*

36. Is it true we don't have any originals of the Bible?

- *Yes, nor of any individual Bible book. However, we have 5,700 copies of all or parts of the NT in Greek. If you examine and compare them, they compare at a level of 95% accuracy. It is not unusual that originals of ancient books do not exist. They were mainly oral cultures and had no printing or copying mechanisms other than manual. The Bible has more copies of manuscripts that are from the closest times to that of the actual events than any other ancient document by far.*

37. **Why do Catholics have other books in the Bible we don't?**

   – *Until the 1600's, the Catholic Bible was the same as the Protestant Bible. Then they chose to add other works such as Maccabees because they believed the other books to be accurate and inspired. This is highly debatable and from a Protestant view incorrect.*

38. **Does God love people who aren't saved?**

   – *Yes God loves everyone. His actual nature is love and He cannot not love someone regardless of how good or bad they are or even if they reject Him. This is the distinct opposite of Allah, the God of Islam, who hates sinners.*

39. **Is it possible someone who is not a Christian might be in heaven?**

   – *It is possible because we cannot know if someone who has not expressed that they are Christian might secretly be a believer or perhaps even had a vision of Christ and were saved. Only God knows for sure.*

40. **Are aliens real?**

   – *Honestly we do not know the answer to this question. Although it is interesting to contemplate, from the standpoint of Christianity it makes no difference. God created the universe and everything in it so if there are aliens they are created by God and under His jurisdiction. Additionally, scripture tells us Christ died once for all and that includes everywhere. From a science perspective, if there are aliens they will be at least similar to us and be carbon-based beings. No other elements are able to bond molecules the way carbon does. Silicon may be the closest but has been ruled out.*

41. **Will we be able to travel to other worlds like on Star Trek?**

   – *Okay now I know we have left the theology classroom and are into science fiction so let's make this the last one. Interestingly enough, even theoretical physicists say we will likely never be able to leave our solar system from a manned spacecraft perspective. At speeds of 25,000 miles per hour, it would take hundreds of thousands of years to escape our solar system. There are no current ideas about revolutionary types of fuel so the challenge is that the faster you build the space vehicle the more fuel it requires so the bigger it needs to be and therefore the more fuel it needs and so on. Even nuclear fission is not a limitless supply of energy. So until scientists can "warp" space like in Star Trek (remember that worm holes are completely a theoretical science fiction fantasy) it is highly unlikely. Beyond that the behavioral issues with humans over extremely long time periods so far shows dangerous evidence of breakdowns and many issues. Cryogenic sleep for long periods of time is again merely a science fiction fantasy as there is no solution even conceived at this point in time.*

42. Why couldn't Jesus have saved Himself because He was God?

- *It was not God's plan and He submitted Himself to God's will. If Jesus accessed His divine powers then we would not have a Savior and would still be dead in our sins. He sacrificed Himself voluntarily because He loves us.*

43. If Jesus was God how could He die?

- *He died in human form and was resurrected by His divine form. He voluntarily gave Himself up to the sting of death to show He could defeat death while saving humanity for the opportunity to choose salvation.*

44. I don't get the AD/BC thing. Was Jesus born in 0?

- *When the calendars were re-calibrated to honor the history of Jesus, they made an error. We believe Jesus was probably born in 4 BC.*

45. Somebody said it wasn't really three days from when Jesus died to His resurrection.

- *Parts of a day were understood as a 'day' also. So part of Friday, all of Saturday and part of Sunday is three days.*

46. Why couldn't God just pardon/forgive us instead of requiring Jesus' sacrifice?

- *This is because God is also all-just. We are guilty and liable due to our sin. But because God is all-just He cannot forgive sin without addressing his requirement for justice. The shedding of blood through a human but also divine nature satisfies His need for righteous judgment for all people at all times. They need only accept and declare Jesus Savior and Lord.*

47. My uncle says science has disproved God, is that right?

- *No. In fact science has nothing to say about anything supernatural because it is the study of the natural world. By definition the supernatural is outside the boundaries of the natural. Yet some scientists choose to delve into this issue and make false claims and typically make erroneous philosophical statements.*

48. Is there such a thing as the multiverse which answers the issue of fine-tuning?

- *Without getting into too much of the science complexities, the multiverse concept with unique infinite random universes is totally theoretical with no evidence whatsoever. It is an idea without justification. Even if there were such a thing, what then caused the multiverse? So it only moves the problem one level back and still requires an all-powerful, omniscient, eternal, timeless cause, which points to God.*

49. **How can God send people to hell just because they don't believe in Him?**

   – *God does not send people to hell. They send themselves when they reject Christ's offer of salvation by grace through faith. Our sins are what condemn us. The Bible says the wages of sin is death. Yes God did create hell but people choose it themselves. Ironically, even if some are convinced there is a hell, due to their unrighteousness they may still rebel and reject Christ.*

50. **Is God jealous?**

   – *Not in the same way as we understand this human emotion. The Bible does say that God is jealous for us when it comes to not wanting us to worship other gods and idols. But God does not have human emotions like we do. He loves but that is His nature. His jealousy for us is simply His protective nature for us and wanting us to be with Him forever. That is for our benefit. Jealousy as a human emotion comes from selfishness and pride.*

51. **President Obama and others said all religions have a lot of similarities. Does that mean we all worship the same God?**

   – *No we do not all worship the same God. This is a common deception and misperception that because all religions have similarities such as the belief in the golden rule or something similar that we must all worship the same God. However, that is not how you compare two things. You compare the differences. When you examine the core doctrines of all religions including creation, God, man, sin, salvation, heaven, hell and many others you will discover that they contradict. The law of noncontradiction, a universal law of logic, states the universal principal that if two things teach opposites then they cannot both be true at the same time and in the same sense. So all religions cannot be true. They could all be false. But if you examine the evidence and find that Christianity is true, then any religion or philosophy that teaches the opposite must be false. This is why it is so important to share the gospel with others.*

52. **My Muslim friend says Jesus did not die, is that true?**

   – *Jesus did die and it is confirmed by all published Biblical scholars, Christian and otherwise and documented in the Bible. It is a false belief by Islam that Christ did not die and is not based on any evidence other than the Qur'an says so. But the Qur'an is not historically reliable and was created out of a vision by a human who did no miracles, did not claim to be God, and was highly sinful. It was created out of a vision when he thought he was being visited by demons. There were no eyewitnesses.*

53. My Muslim friend says we worship 3 Gods, is that true?

– *No, we worship one God who exists in three persons. God has one nature but expresses Himself in three persons: the Father, the Son and the Holy Spirit, referred to as the Trinity. Deuteronomy 6:4 declares God is one. But the three persons of the Trinity all have the characteristics of God including omnipotence, omniscience, and omnipresence.*

54. My Muslim friend says Moses was a Muslim, is that true?

– *No this is a deceptive belief by Muslims to try and claim that they worship the God of the Bible and that they are descendants of Moses and that Moses was a Muslim. Sometimes it is also stated as Abraham instead. It is true that Abraham had his first son with his wife's servant and the son was named Ishmael. Ishmael was banished by God and God's covenant was established with Isaac instead, a son he had with his wife Sarah at age 100. Ishmael left for the Middle East and a descendant ultimately birthed Mohammed and Islam was formed through him. Then another descendnt of Ishmael married an Edomite woman (descendant of Esau) and there has been hatred of Jews by Arabs ever since. Ironically it might be more accurate to say that Muslims come from a Jewish line.*

55. My Muslim friend says the bible is corrupt and has lots of errors, is that true?

– *No the Bible is historically reliable and errors are spelling, typos and copying errors mainly. Islam makes this claim to dispute the accuracy of the Bible and justify their contradictory doctrines in the Qur'an. They claim that somewhere along the way the Bible was corrupted and that the New Testament today is not the original recording. However, the Bible we have today compares to better than 95% accuracy with the Bibles available at the time the Qur'an and Mohammed existed, around AD 600. So ask the Muslim when it was corrupted and where is their evidence? It is merely a hollow claim because they want to discredit the Bible and claim the Qur'an has the truth. Ironically, the Qur'an itself commands its readers to turn to the Injil (New Testament) to know the truth.*

56. President Obama and others say Islam is a religion of peace, is that right?

– *This is a far too broad and deceptive statement. In fact the President actually said in a speech once that the word Islam comes from the Arabic word for peace. This is a total falsehood. The word Islam means "submit" in Arabic, not peace. There are Muslims who are peaceful; no doubt the majority. But Islam itself is not a religion of peace in any way. Islam has been responsible for more deaths than any dictator in history. The early verses of the Qur'an which seem to indicate some peaceful passages are abrogated (updated/replaced) by later verses. What really happened is that when Mohammed began his preaching in a peaceful way no one listened and he had no more than a handful of followers. Coincidentally, he claims to have received new visions and commands from Allah at that time that encouraged him to use force. From that time on he developed an army and became a vicious, immoral and unethical military leader and conquered countries throughout the Middle East and Europe. At issue is the Qur'anic word jihad. It means "struggle". Many Muslims will say the meaning of the struggle is like an inner strife and so they reject the claims of others who say jihad means Holy War and physical violence. But of the 150 or so verses in the Qur'an that mention the word jihad, about 100 refer to external jihad, which is violent Holy War.*

57. I heard a scientist say faith is foolish. Is that right?

– Faith that is based on reason and evidence is not foolish. This claim by some scientists and other nonbelievers is based on the false assumption that faith means believing in something without evidence; or blind faith. No that is not what Christians believe. Our faith is based on substantial evidence from science, nature, history and philosophy that points directly to the existence of God, reliability of the Bible, and resurrection of Jesus. We know from the Bible in proverbs that "the fool says there is no God." So the opposite is actually true. To ignore the significant evidence that God exists even from nature is to deny reality and is foolish. Romans 1:18 explains it is due to our unrighteousness that they suppress the truth.

58. I heard the Bible is filled with hundreds of thousands of errors. Is that right?

– Technically, it is correct that there are many spelling and copying errors. But the important thing to understand is almost none of them affect any actual meaning of the scripture and none affect any important doctrines. When a scribe copied a manuscript it had to be done manually. Imagine yourself copying a book of the Bible flawlessly. Over centuries some errors were made. But also, deceptively, the way critics count errors is by taking one error in a manuscript and multiplying it by the number of manuscript copies. We have 5,700 Greek NT manuscripts in full or partial so one error in one could be counted as 5,700 if it appears in all of them. It is also important to know there are places in the NT in particular where some passages are included in today's Bible that may not be in the earliest manuscripts. But if you look at the notes at the bottom of the page it is always disclosed. In some cases scribes may not have been sure whether the spelling they were reading meant one word or a very similar word with a different character. So those are possibilities. The Bible has been proven to be over 95% accurate, more than any ancient writing by far.

59. Why do we have all the different Bible versions?

- *As language evolves, some words are no longer relevant in today's society. For example, no one speaks in the Shakespearian type language of the King James Version any more. Also, Bibles are written either word for word, captured thought, or a combination. From one language to another it is not always possible to make a word for word translation that makes sense to someone in another language.*

60. I heard something about other books of the Bible that weren't included. Why not?

- *We call the books that were included the 'canon'. Decisions were made around the mid –AD 300's based on known commonly accepted books used, ones written by prophets, ones written by apostles, or ones written by trusted reporters who interviewed apostles. So all decisions were based on a reliability of the known author seen as an inspired messenger of God or at least accepted scripture by the majority at the time. Some of the so-called 'apocrypha' books not included were forgeries or written by apostasy writers who contradicted many of Jesus' main teachings so they were known to be false.*

61. Is there any source outside the Bible to verify it is true?

- *Yes, actually the entire NT is recorded in external writings except for about four verses of John. We have several million quotes from the NT by teachers and other authors, many of which are also non-Christian sources.*

62. I heard that Muslims and Hindu really believe their religion is true. Can that be right?

- *Unfortunately not if Christianity is true. Other religions contradict core doctrine so both cannot be true. The universal law of logic called the Law of Noncontradiction excludes two things being true that teach opposites. So we must examine the evidence. When you do, you will find the other religions lack historical, verifiable evidence and eyewitness support. Christianity does have that.*

63. If we evolved from apes, why are there still apes around?

- *This is a common misunderstanding by many Christian children and perhaps some adults. It refers to the Darwinian evolutionary claim that both apes and humans had a common ancestor that created us. But some children have the idea in their heads that it means apes turned into humans and then there were no apes anymore. Although the common descent ancestry of apes and humans bears no evidence or proof other than an assumption, it does not* mean Darwinists are saying that apes turned into humans. What they are saying is that some ancestor had descendants that were apes and others that became human. But that is also based on assumptions with no proof.

64. Who created God?

– My great nephew asked me this question when he was about five years old. The answer is no one made God. God is self-existent. He is not self-caused which is a logical contradiction. He is uncaused. God is the uncaused first cause of all other causes. If you think about this using common sense and work backwards, you can quickly see that this must be the case. I teach the kids this way: let's say that the universe was created by A. Then who created A? Let's say it was B. Then take this through the alphabet and when you get to the question, "Who created Z?" you say it was A1. Then they understand it could go on infinitely but that actually it not only makes no sense but is logically impossible and called an infinite regression. There must be a first cause which is uncaused in order to prevent the infinite regression. That uncaused first cause is God.

APOLOGETICS FOR TWEENS
5TH GRADE LESSON CURRICULUM
THOMAS J. GRIFFIN
June 2017

ATHANATOS
PUBLISHING GROUP
www.athanatos.org